ROBERT and ELIZABETH

A New Musical

from an original idea by Fred G. Morritt

Based on *The Barretts of Wimpole Street*
by RUDOLPH BESIER

Book and Lyrics by RONALD MILLAR

Music by RON GRAINER

SAMUEL FRENCH

LONDON

NEW YORK   SYDNEY   TORONTO   HOLLYWOOD

PRINTED IN GREAT BRITAIN
BY W & J MACKAY & CO LTD, CHATHAM

ROBERT AND ELIZABETH

Presented by Martin Landau for Marlan Productions Ltd, at the Lyric Theatre, London, on the 20th October 1964, with the following cast of characters:

(in order of their appearance)

VENDORS	*Perry Johnson, Dean Viner*
POLICEMEN	*Bryon O'Leary, David Sinclair*
SWEEPER	*Charles West*
POSTMEN	*Ken Robson, Patrick McIntyre*
LAMPLIGHTER	*Alan Dudley*
WORKING BOYS	*Rex Rainer, Louis Godfrey*
CHLOE	*Jill Love*
CLAIRE	*Patsy Porter*
A PICKPOCKET	*David Kelsey*
EDWARD MOULTON-BARRETT	*John Clements*
HENRIETTA	*Angela Richards*
ARABEL	*Mary Denison*
GEORGE	*John Tillinger*
ALFRED	*Rod McLennan*
HENRY	*John McGee*
CHARLES	*Ivor Danvers*
SEPTIMUS	*John Parker*
OCTAVIUS	*Michael Ridgeway*
BELLA HEDLEY	*Sarah Badel*
HENRY BEVAN	*Gordon Wilcox*
CAPTAIN SURTEES COOK	*Jeremy Lloyd*
A FELLOW OFFICER	*David Jennings*
WILSON	*Stella Moray*
FLUSH	*Dewcroft Pandora*
DOCTOR CHAMBERS	*Charles West*
ELIZABETH	*June Bronhill*
MR MACREADY	*David Kelsey*
MR HARRISON, King Charles	*Bryon O'Leary*
STAGE MANAGER, Mr Langton	*Alan Dudley*
MRS BUTLER, Polyxena	*Cynthia Morey*
EVANS	*Robert Vahey*
ROBERT BROWNING	*Keith Michell*
TRAVERS	*Alan Dudley*
LADY MARY	*Barbara Leigh*
LADY SARAH	*Cynthia Morey*
SANDWICH-BOARD MAN	*Alan Dudley*

SINGERS: Barbara Leigh, Cynthia Morey, Catherine Snedden, Jennifer Conway, Marilyn Dougan, Anita Lockwood, Wendy Eathorne, David Jennings, Dean Viner, Perry Johnson, David Sinclair, Bryon O'Leary, Gordon Wilcox.

DANCERS: Jill Love, Judith Eltham, Patsy Porter, Pamela Miller, Ruth Till, Rex Rainer, Louis Godfrey, Patrick McIntyre, Ken Robson, Arthur Sweet.

NOTES ON STAGING

This Acting Edition describes the way in which the musical was staged at the Lyric Theatre, London. It is realized that amateur companies will not necessarily have the stage facilities enabling them exactly to conform with the mechanics of staging described—they are set out as an ideal at which to aim.

Without doubt each producer will draw on experience and knowledge of local stage conditions to arrive at an individual solution to the problems, in conjunction with the scenic contractor, stage manager and crew concerned.

Notes for a simplified running sequence will be found on page 107. These may help to suggest the simplest answer to your own particular difficulties.

The Sets

The play calls for five full-stage sets, each used once only:

The Vicinity of Wimpole Street.
The (almost bare) Stage of the Theatre Royal, Haymarket.
The Garden of 50 Wimpole Street.
Cremorne Gardens, Chelsea.
Vauxhall Station/Florence Station.

There are two in-sets, each used four times:

The Hallway of 50 Wimpole Street.
Elizabeth's Bedroom.

And one front-drop:

Outside Browning's Study.

The simplified running sequence also employs one set of neutral running tabs.

It is important that the two in-sets are light, easily handled, and simple to erect and strike. Trucking is ideal. It must be possible to build and strike the Bedroom inside the Hallway without striking the Hallway. In the simplified running plan the building time allowed for in-set changes is about one minute.

SYNOPSIS OF SCENES

The action of the play passes in the BARRETT *home in Wimpole Street, and various parts of London during the years 1845 and 1846.*

ACT I

SCENE 1   The Vicinity of Wimpole Street
SCENE 2   The Hall of No. 50 Wimpole Street
SCENE 3   Elizabeth's Room
SCENE 4   The Stage of the Theatre Royal, Haymarket
SCENE 5   Elizabeth's Room
SCENE 6   The Hall of No. 50 Wimpole Street
SCENE 7   The Garden of No. 50 Wimpole Street

ACT II

SCENE 1   Elizabeth's Room
SCENE 2   The Hall of No. 50 Wimpole Street
SCENE 3   Cremorne Gardens, Chelsea
SCENE 4   The Hall of No. 50 Wimpole Street
SCENE 5   Elizabeth's Room
SCENE 6   Outside Browning's Study
SCENE 7   Vauxhall Station
SCENE 8   Florence

MUSICAL CONTENTS

ACT I

ACT II

ACT I

SCENE I

OVERTURE

No. I

The Vicinity of Wimpole Street. Evening

Four lamp-posts extend diagonally from up C *to down* L. *Down* R *is a chestnut brazier with a tray of chestnuts. On either side of the brazier are baskets, one of fruit, one of tomatoes. Throughout the stylized opening scene, an impressionistic view of this part of fashionable London in the year eighteen forty-five is gradually revealed.*

When the CURTAIN *rises, three* STREET VENDORS *are discovered round the brazier, singing their wares. Two* POLICEMEN *stand down* RC *and* LC, *and two groups of* ELEGANT LADIES *up* L *and* L.

OPENING STREET SCENE

No. 2

STREET VENDORS.
> Red hot chestnuts!
> Ripe bananas!

(*A* CROSSING SWEEPER *enters up* R)

> Fresh tomatoes!
> And apple 'n pears!

(*A* LAMPLIGHTER *enters up* R. *An* ELEGANT LADY *and* GENTLEMAN *enter down* R *and cross up* L)

POLICEMEN.
> Here on the corner of Wimpole Street
> Oxford Street and Cavendish Square

(*The* LAMPLIGHTER *lights the upstage lamp then the other three*)

> Lighting up time is at six tonight
> Nice and bright
> The glitter and glare
> Floods over the Square.

(*The* POLICEMEN *move up* L. *The* SWEEPER *moves down* C)

SWEEPER (*sweeping away*)
> Just got it tidy in Wimpole Street
> Oxford Street and Cavendish Square
> Then comes a couple of horses through

(*The* SWEEPER *moves down* R. *Two* POSTMEN *enter down* L)

> I ask you

Look at that over there
Don't 'arf make you swear.
POSTMEN.
Everyone wants to communicate
SWEEPER.
Nobody wants to be clean

(*The* CROSSING SWEEPER *exits down* R. *The* LAMPLIGHTER *comes down* C. *The* ELEGANT LADIES *move down* L)

LAMPLIGHTER.
Doing my bit to illuminate

(*The* POSTMEN *move upstage*)

The Victorian scene
As safe and serene
As the World's ever been.

(*The* LAMPLIGHTER *exits down* R. *The* ELEGANT LADY DANCERS *move down* C)

ELEGANT LADIES.
Elegant ladies of Wimpole Street
Oxford Street and Cavendish Square
Find it a pleasure to ambulate
Circulate
Our nose in the air
We appear to declare
We're the only—

(*A group of* ROUGH BOY *and* GIRL DANCERS *enter up* R *and move down* C, *followed by a* BARMAID *with a bar to* C. *The* LAMPLIGHTER *enters down* R *with a dartboard. The* VENDORS *exit down* R *with the brazier and baskets*)

—ones there.
WORKING BOYS AND GIRLS.
'Oo gives a pfft about Wimpole Street
Oxford Street or Cavendish Square?
Ruddy sight rather 'ave Befnal Green—

(SURTEES COOK *and a* FELLOW OFFICER *enter down* L *to* L *of the line of rough people*)

Parson's Green or Wapping Old Stairs
Than all of your Squares.

(*The* POSTMEN *play darts.* OTHERS *drink at the bar. The* ELEGANT LADIES *and* GENTLEMEN *move* LC. *The* GUARDS OFFICERS *move up* L, *making room for the* ROUGH BOYS *and* GIRLS *to dance* C)

After the work of the day is through
Me and the boys have a pint or two

Then we're all set for a 'owdyoudo
With Chloe or Clare.
Look beautiful bare,
Do Chloe and Clare
THREE ELEGANT LADIES (*spoken*) Disgusting!

(*The bar is pushed off up* R)

LAMPLIGHTER.
Cor, what hips, mate
STREET VENDOR.
Red hot chestnuts!
LAMPLIGHTER.
Red hot lips, mate
2ND WORKING LAD.
You've got something there
3RD WORKING LAD.
Especially Clare.

(*There is ribald laughter. The lamp-posts are moved to form a square with the brazier in the centre. The* LAMPLIGHTER *takes the dartboard off down* L *then joins the group of rough people at the brazier* C. *The* POLICE *move down* R *and down* L)

POLICEMAN.
No criminal classes in Wimpole—

(*A* PICKPOCKET *enters* RC)

—Street
Oxford Street or Cavendish Square.

PICKPOCKET (*stealing a wallet and purses from an* ELEGANT GENTLEMAN *and two* ELEGANT LADIES *by the lamp-posts down* R *and down* L)

Nickin' a wad from a well-to-do
Swell-to-do
Well, it's sort of a flair—

(*He avoids the Policeman down* L *and comes down* C)

'Course, you got to take care.
POLICEMAN.
Seems quiet everywhere.
PICKPOCKET (*spoken*) Mind, to make a dishonest living you've got to know your territory. Me, I know Wimpole Street like I know the Scrubs.
At number twenty-six
There's Sir Geoffrey Johnson-'Icks
Who's Apothecary-General to the Queen.
STREET VENDORS. Red hot chestnuts!
PICKPOCKET (*spoken*)
At number thirty-eight

There's a shiny dental plate
And there's 'arf the Docs in England in between.
STREET VENDORS. Ripe bananas!
PICKPOCKET (*spoken*)
    Number forty-one's
    Got a lawyer and his son—
STREET VENDORS. Fresh tomatoes!
PICKPOCKET (*spoken*)
    And at number fifty—Wow!
    'Ere's Mr Barrett now.

(*The* PICKPOCKET *joins the group at the brazier* C. *The* POLICE-
MEN *move upstage.* EDWARD MOULTON-BARRETT *enters up* R,
followed by HENRIETTA, ARABEL, OCTAVIUS, SEPTIMUS, HENRY,
CHARLES, ALFRED *and* GEORGE, *all in single file. They are
severely dressed in black and carry prayer-books and bibles.* BARRETT
*wears a top hat and frock coat. Led by their father, looking neither to
right nor left, they proceed gravely round the Square. They cross
upstage to* L, *then circle downstage towards down* R, *forming a line
downstage.* BELLA HEDLEY *and* HENRY BEVAN *enter down* R,
meeting BARRETT *down* RC. BELLA *is voluble, affected and exquisitely
pretty, with a constitutional inability to pronounce her R's.* BEVAN *is
stiff, pompous and extremely rich.* BELLA *curtsys to Barrett and
introduces her fiancé. The* FAMILY, *one by one, greet Bevan and Bella,
raising their hats or curtsying. The music becomes suddenly military
in tempo, as* SURTEES COOK *marches from down* L *in front of the
brothers and tries to give a note to Henrietta.* BARRETT, *who is
talking to Bella, turns and sees him.* COOK *retreats to down* L, *then
marches behind the brothers preceded by the* FELLOW OFFICER, *who
obstructs Barrett's view while* COOK *puts the note in Henrietta's
prayer-book. Both* OFFICERS *then cross to down* L. *The* SISTERS *and
BROTHERS cross below Barrett and exit down* R, *bowing or raising
their hats as they pass. The* OFFICERS *try to follow, but* BARRETT
glares at them. The OFFICERS *turn and exit down* L. BARRETT *exits
down* R. BELLA *and* BEVAN *move down* C. WILSON, *a long-suffering
Lady's Maid, enters up* L *with* FLUSH *on a lead, and comes down* C)

WILSON.
    Dragged by a spaniel up Wimpole Street
    Oxford Street, round Cavendish Square
    Should be all right if you take it slow
    All I know
    The wear and the tear
    Is greying me hair
    Somebody taught him to beg at folk
    Up on your lap with a bound
    Next he'll be lifting his leg at folk
    Never knew such a hound

For wetting the ground
He'll have us all drowned.

(WILSON and FLUSH move down R. An ELEGANT LADY comes
down from beside the lamp-post to L of Wilson, admiringly)

ELEGANT LADY (spoken) Excuse me, what a sweet little dog.
What do they call him?
WILSON (spoken) Flush, madam—and no wonder.

(WILSON and FLUSH exit down R. The ROUGH BOYS and POST-
MEN move the lamp-posts into a line against the back-cloth. The
SINGERS come into line downstage. SURTEES COOK and his FELLOW
OFFICER enter down L and join the line: VENDOR, ELEGANT LADY,
ELEGANT LADY, POLICEMAN, ELEGANT LADY, VENDOR, BEVAN,
BELLA, ELEGANT LADY, PICKPOCKET, BARMAID, VENDOR,
LAMPLIGHTER, ELEGANT LADY, POLICEMAN, ELEGANT LADY,
SURTEES COOK, FELLOW OFFICER. The daylight is fading)

FULL ENSEMBLE.
        Night is descending on Wimpole Street
        Oxford Street and Cavendish Square
        What a salubrious neighbourhood
        All that's good
        And noble and fair
        Is resident there
        Morally based on the family
        Britain is certain to thrive
        Oh, what a marvellous century
        For being alive
        What a year to arrive
LAMPLIGHTER.
        Eighteen forty-five
FULL ENSEMBLE.
        Up the Empire!
        Queen and Country!
        Horse and buggy!
        Nice 'n Easy!

(The LINE begins to move upstage)

        Fam'ly Circle!
        Peaceful England!
        Eighteen forty-five
        Eighteen forty-five
        Eighteen forty-five

(The VOICES die away, the LIGHTS fade on the scene, and we are
in—

Scene 2

The Hall of Number Fifty, Wimpole Street

It is a typically Victorian interior, heavy with mahogany and rosewood and gas chandeliers. Signs of the head of the household's earlier years in Jamaica mingle with the Victoriana. There is a fireplace L, and an alcove R in which is a harmonium. At the back a staircase leads off L to the rest of the house. Facing the staircase is a front door. Up C is a door to the library. The general impression is of affluence rather than opulence and, despite the large open area of the hall, the house strikes immediately as oppressive.

As the scene changes and the Lights *go up the* Brothers *and* Sisters *enter to their places:* Henrietta *to sit down* L *with needlework,* George *to sit above the fire.* Henry *and* Alfred *with chairs and a chess-board to sit up* RC *and play.* Arabel *to sit at the harmonium,* Charles, Septimus *and* Octavius *with hymn-books to stand round* Arabel *and sing.*

"LOVE AND DUTY"   No. 3

Arabel
Charles
Septimus
Octavius
} Love and duty fill this house—

(Barrett *enters up* R, *moves up* C, *takes letters from the table up* C, *and moves down* C)

Warm the wainscote
Heat the hearth
Bar the door to hate and guile—

(Wilson *enters downstairs and moves* L *of Barrett*)

Envy with her mocking laugh.

(*The* Music *continues*)

Wilson. Shall I take Miss Elizabeth's letter, sir?

(Barrett *looks up slowly from going through the mail*)

It's Friday, sir.

(Barrett *stares at Wilson coldly*)

There's always a letter on Friday, sir.

(Barrett *stares at her a moment longer, then hands her a letter in silence*)

Thank you, sir. (*She moves to the stairs*)

(Dr Chambers *enters downstairs, meeting Wilson at the foot. He is an elderly bewhiskered man, carrying a black medical bag*)

Doctor.

(WILSON *exits upstairs.* ARABEL *stops playing*)

BARRETT (*moving to the fire-place*) Well, Dr Chambers?

CHAMBERS. There's no great change, sir.

BARRETT. By which florid statement I take it you mean there's no change of any kind, for better or worse.

CHAMBERS. Where the very nature of the illness remains an enigma one hardly expects it, Mr Barrett.

BARRETT. In that case your constant visits to my daughter— to say nothing of your constant fees to me—would seem to lack purpose.

CHAMBERS. One must examine, Mr Barrett. One must probe.

BARRETT. One must pray, sir. Since your ministrations have so little effect we can only pray to Almighty God that she may fix her heart and soul on Him and on that Heavenly Eternity which may at any moment open out before her.

CHAMBERS. Come, sir, let's not anticipate. She's still a young woman. And for someone who's been confined to one room for years on end, her brain is quite astonishingly active. Her Greek studies, her articles for the Athenaeum—

(BARRETT *looks through the letters and hands three to George.* GEORGE *rises and goes to give the letters to Henry and Charles*)

—not to mention her poetry—a remarkable output. I can't help feeling that if only we could get her out of England . . .

(*The* BROTHERS *and* SISTERS *look up in surprise*)

BARRETT. Out of England? Are you aware, sir, that my daughter requires help to get out of her bed?

CHAMBERS. Oh quite, quite—an impossible dream. Nevertheless, there's no doubt that a move to a warmer climate—away from this house . . .

(CHAMBERS *waves a hand at the encircling gloom, encounters* BARRETT'*s forbidding gaze, and coughs apologetically*)

BARRETT. This house is her home, sir. Her permanent home.

CHAMBERS (*quickly*) Yes, indeed. And it's delightful. Most pleasing. Quite charming. I'll look in again next week as usual. Good night, Mr Barrett, good night to you, sir.

(CHAMBERS *takes his hat and gloves from the table up* C *and* GEORGE *goes to open the door up* R. CHAMBERS *exits.* GEORGE *closes the door and moves up* L)

ARABEL (*beating time*) One, two!

(*The* FAMILY *resume their hymn.* BARRETT *places the remaining letters on the mantelpiece*)

THE FAMILY.
Love and duty fill this house
Warm the wainscote, heat the hearth
BARRETT. May I have your attention, please?
OCTAVIUS (*singing*)
Bar the door to hate and guile . . .

BARRETT. Forgive the interruption, Octavius. Would you care to entertain us further?
OCTAVIUS (*who stammers, especially under stress*) N-n-no, sir. (*He moves away down* RC)
BARRETT. In that case, with your permission. (*He addresses the family in measured tones*) I have to tell you that for the third consecutive Friday, on our return from Chapel, I observed a certain military officer pass by us, almost as it were by prior arrangement, in close proximity and at the identical spot.

(*There is a silence*)

The officer appeared to be not unknown to a certain member of this family. I invite that member to step forward.

(*There is another silence. At length* ALFRED *rises and moves* RC)

ALFRED. Captain Cook is a friend of mine, sir.

(OCTAVIUS *moves* R *of Alfred.* HENRY *rises, holding the chessboard*)

OCTAVIUS. And m-mine, sir.
BARRETT (*moving to Alfred; musing*) The identical spot, three Fridays running—and just for a sight of Alfred and Octavius. (*He inspects them closely, as if to find a clue to their secret fascination*) Remarkable. A rare devotion. I had the distinct impression that this Captain Cook was endeavouring to communicate in a clandestine manner with Henrietta—

(HENRIETTA *rises.* BARRETT *turns to her*)

—and she with him. Had that been so, I need hardly tell you I should have been very gravely displeased. However, it seems that I was mistaken. (*He looks from Alfred to Octavius to Henrietta, and raps out*) Was I?
ALFRED. Yes, sir.
BARRETT. Was I?
OCTAVIUS. Y-yes, sir.
BARRETT (*very softly*) Was I?
HENRIETTA. Yes, Papa.
BARRETT (*after a pause*) Very well. I have no alternative but to accept the combined word of three of my children—a triple lie being out of the question.

(ARABEL *gives an odd strangled noise*)

Was that an observation, Arabel, or have you dyspepsia?

Arabel (*faintly*) N-no, Papa.

Barrett. Then don't grunt when I'm speaking. (*He addresses them all*) Since a regular view of Alfred and Octavius, though doubtless rewarding, is not, so far as I am aware, considered essential to mental health, I shall expect *not* to encounter the ubiquitous Captain as a postscript to next Friday's devotions, or, indeed, on any future itinerary. Do I make myself sufficiently clear?

All ⎱ Very clear, sir.
⎰ Yes, Papa.
⎰ Yes, sir.

Barrett. Then there is no more to be said. (*He moves to the foot of the stairs then turns*) Pray continue your musical evening— with a clear conscience.

(Barrett *exits upstairs*)

"THE FAMILY MOULTON-BARRETT"   No. 4

(*The* Family *watch* Barrett *exit. Somewhere above a door slams. The* Family *form a group:* Alfred *in the small chair up* c, Henry *and* Charles *standing above him,* George *standing up* lc, Octavius *above the fire-place,* Henrietta *sitting below the fire,* Arabel *sitting by the harmonium,* Septimus *standing above her*)

All.   Schooled in filial piety
              Safe from the perils of Victorian society
              Father preserves us under lock and key
              Others may risk their spiritual necks
              Getting involved with the opposite sex
              Not we
              Most emphatically no, not we

George.
              From every conceivable passion
              From every improbable vice

Charles.
              From some that are thoroughly nasty

Alfred. And a few that are really rather nice

All.   He shields his flock
              He's a rock
              Yes, morally our father is a rock!

Septimus.
              If one of us should eye
              A girl

Arabel. Or boy

Henry. Or experience a momentary passing joy
              He would die

All.   Yes, he'd die!
              He'd unquestionably die—
              Of shock.

(The Family *form another group:* Alfred *rises and moves his chair up* lc, Henry *moves the other chair up* rc. Henrietta *sits up* lc, Arabel *up* rc. Henry *stands* r *of Arabel,* Alfred *above her,* Charles *stands* l *of Henrietta,* George *above her.* Septimus *sits on the floor below Arabel,* Octavius *below Henrietta)*

  We think as one, we act as one
Septimus.
  We never do what should not be done
All. And we blench if you mention good clean fun
  In the family Moulton-Barrett
Sisters. Mama was sweet
Octavius ⎱
Septimus ⎰ Papa's severe
George.
  Mama passed on
Alfred. Papa's still here
Charles.
  The ways of Providence are not quite clear
All. To the family Moulton-Barrett

(The Sisters *rise and move down* l *and down* r, *holding their hands over their ears)*

Brothers.
  Sex is not permissible
  If you're kissable
  Kindly go away.

*(*Charles *and* Henry *take hold of the* Sisters, *who push them away)*

Charles *and* Henry *(together)*
  We may not take hold of you
Sisters. Oh, how bold of you!
Arabel. He asked me for a Polka!
George.
  We're always calm—we never fuss
Arabel. I *would* like a big man's hair to muss

*(*Henrietta *crosses* r *to Arabel)*

Brothers.
  The sins of the flesh are not for us
All. The family Moulton-Barrett
  Whatever we do, whatever we say
  There's one strict rule we all obey:
Alfred *and* Charles *(together)*
  "No one gets in the family way"
  In the family Moulton-Barrett.

(*The* FAMILY *form another group:* HENRIETTA *stands down* R, SEPTIMUS L *of and slightly above her, then, in order to down* L— OCTAVIUS, ARABEL, HENRY, GEORGE, ALFRED, CHARLES)

OCTAVIUS, HENRIETTA *and* SEPTIMUS (*together*)
    Wicked cousin Caroline
    Dared to take a shine
    To a certain man
CHARLES.
    What's more, having wed with him
ALFRED. Went to bed with him.

(ARABEL *faints into* HENRY's *arms*)

GEORGE. Arabel has fainted!
CHARLES.
    "Tempt them, Devil!"
    Papa once cried
SEPTIMUS *and* OCTAVIUS (*together*)
    "We're eager to be tempted"
    We replied
GEORGE, ALFRED *and* HENRY (*together*)
    But the Devil just shrugged his horns and sighed
    (*miming*) "It's the family Moulton-Barrett"
CHARLES.
    What with conscience pricking us
SEPTIMUS.
    Father kicking us
    Firmly in the rear
GEORGE.
    We stay starkly celibate
ALFRED. Scared to pick a mate
    And propagate the species

(GEORGE *and* ALFRED *kneel down* C. ALL *hold their hands as though praying*)

ALL.   Onward, Moulton-Barretts!
    Down with Heaven's foes!
OCTAVIUS.
    How we ever got here Heaven only knows
HENRIETTA, ARABEL, SEPTIMUS, OCTAVIUS *and* HENRY (*together*)
    We love Papa, revere Papa
    Oh dear, oh dear, oh dear Papa
GEORGE, ALFRED *and* CHARLES (*together*)
    He really is a very, very queer Papa
ALL.   Is Edward Moulton-Barrett

(*They take up the following positions in line* L *to* R: ARABEL, HENRIETTA, SEPTIMUS, OCTAVIUS, HENRY, *then after a space,* CHARLES, GEORGE, ALFRED)

ALFRED *and* CHARLES (*together*)
    We've learnt our Bibles backwards
SISTERS.
    We're demurely polite and prim
    (*moving down* LC) But, golly, it's lonely
    When Chapel's the only
    Sight you get of a him
BROTHERS.
    Or her
SISTERS. The only sight of a him!

(*They form another group:* SEPTIMUS L *of the harmonium,* OCTAVIUS L *of Septimus,* ARABEL *in the chair* RC, HENRIETTA *in the chair* LC, ALFRED *seated below the fire-place,* GEORGE *standing* R *of the fire-place,* HENRY *above Arabel,* CHARLES *above Henrietta*)

ALL.   When we're told that we can't go dancing
    We would frequently like to scream—
ARABEL. Aah!
OCTAVIUS.
    But then we recall
    Though we're missing the b-ball
    We're almost a c-cricket team
ALL.   Heigh-ho, Life's a bagatelle
    Love's a carousel
    Dearly love a ride
ALFRED. Says our saintly patriarch
    Straight from Noah's Ark
GEORGE.
    "Riding is Verboten"

(*They line up downstage, from* R *to* L: OCTAVIUS, ALFRED, HENRY, HENRIETTA, CHARLES, ARABEL, SEPTIMUS, GEORGE)

CHARLES.
    Well, one thing's clear
HENRY. The past is past
SEPTIMUS.
    If someone doesn't do something fast
GEORGE.
    You're looking at the positively final cast
ALL *except* OCTAVIUS (*pointing at him*)
    You will be the last, my son
HENRIETTA, HENRY, ALFRED, CHARLES *and* OCTAVIUS (*together*)
    Of the formerly fertile
    Presently thrifty

(*They form a group:* OCTAVIUS R, ALFRED L *of him,* HENRIETTA *below the chair* RC, CHARLES *below the chair* LC, HENRY, SEPTIMUS, GEORGE, *then* ARABEL *seated on the seat below the fire-place*)

ARABEL, GEORGE *and* SEPTIMUS *(together)*
     Currently-domiciled-at-number-fifty
ALL.   Moulton-Barretts of Wimpole Street
     West
OCTAVIUS *and* ALFRED *(together)*
     One!
HENRIETTA *and* CHARLES *(together)*
     A-Two
SEPTIMUS *and* HENRY *(together)*
     A-Three
GEORGE *and* ARABEL *(together)*
     A-Four
ALL.   The formerly fruitful
     Rapidly shrinking
CHARLES.
     Wouldn't-it-be-heaven-to-get-absolutely-stinking
ALL.   Moulton-Barretts of Wimpole Street, Oxford Street
     And Cavendish Square,
     West One!

ALL *move upstage,* CHARLES *and* GEORGE *taking the chairs with them, as the* LIGHTS *fade.*

SCENE CHANGE MUSIC   No.
                            4a

SCENE 3

ELIZABETH'S *bed-sitting room. Evening*

It is a claustrophobic room, the windows papered over to keep out all possible draught, the blinds and curtains drawn. The colours of some items of furnishing are referred to in the lyrics to Musical No. 5, and these should be observed. The room is lit by lamplight. There is a door from the landing up RC. *Above and to* L *of it is a four-poster bed, and* R *is a green baize door to Barrett's bedroom. There are busts of Chaucer and Homer, and books and medicine bottles in profusion.*

When the LIGHTS *go up,* ELIZABETH *is discovered lying on a sofa, her feet covered with a couvre-pied. On her lap is a tray with a largely unfinished meal on it. Below the sofa is a table with an opened letter. On another table, is an unfinished game of patience.* FLUSH, *the dog, lies on the end of the sofa.* WILSON *is tidying the desk* R. ELIZABETH *has a tankard of porter to her lips, which she is manfully trying to swallow. She lowers the tankard with a grimace.*

ELIZABETH. It's no use, I can't. I simply *cannot!* Take it away, Wilson.

WILSON *(moving to the chair* L *of the table* C*)* Try again, miss.

ELIZABETH. Take it away!

WILSON (*moving above the sofa*) Miss, you know it's the master's strict instructions.

ELIZABETH. Will you or won't you take away that horrible black beer?

(*There is a knock on the door*)

Come in.

(OCTAVIUS *enters up* RC)

WILSON (*taking the tankard and moving* L *of the sofa to put it on the table below; disapprovingly*) P'raps you'll try again later, miss.

ELIZABETH. Hello, Occy dear.

OCTAVIUS (*moving above the sofa*) J-just came to see how you are and wish you g-good night. (*He bends down and kisses her*) Doctor satisfied?

ELIZABETH. Oh yes, I think so.

(*There is a knock at the door.* OCTAVIUS *moves up to the bed alcove.* WILSON *moves up to* L *of Octavius*)

Come in.

(SEPTIMUS *enters*)

SEPTIMUS (*moving above the sofa*) How are you, Ba? (*He kisses her*) I hope the Doctor is satisfied with you?

ELIZABETH. Oh yes, I think so.

(SEPTIMUS *moves to the window down* L *and takes a sweet from the dish on the dresser*)

Wilson, has Flush had his dinner?

WILSON. I'm taking him now, miss.

ELIZABETH (*feeding the dog from her plate*) Here. Good boy, good boy.

WILSON. That's not his, that's yours, miss. (*She takes the tray from Elizabeth*) Oh miss, you've hardly touched it.

ELIZABETH. I'm not hungry.

WILSON (*moving up* C *with the tray and taking the dog*) Come along, Flush.

(WILSON *and* FLUSH *exit up* C. ALFRED *knocks on the door*)

ELIZABETH. Come in, Alfred.

ALFRED (*moving above the sofa*) And how's our Ba tonight? Doctor happy?

ELIZABETH. Oh yes, I think so.

(ALFRED *sits* L *of the table* C *and plays with the cards. There is a knock on the door*)

Come in, Henry.

(HENRY *enters*)

HENRY (*moving above the sofa*) How are you feeling tonight, old girl? (*He kisses her*) I hope the doctor's report was good?
ELIZABETH. Oh yes, I think so.

(HENRY *moves to the bookcase up* R *and reads a book. There is a knock on the door*)
Come in, Charles.

(CHARLES *enters*)

CHARLES (*moving above the sofa*) Well, and how's the patient? Doctor pleased with you?
ELIZABETH. Oh yes, I think so.

(*There is a knock on the door*)
Come in, George.

(GEORGE *enters, followed by* HENRIETTA *and* ARABEL. GEORGE *moves above the sofa*, R *of Charles*)

GEORGE. Evening, Ba. (*He kisses her*) Doctor's been, hasn't he? What did he say?
ELIZABETH. Oh yes, I think so. I mean—I'm much the same, dear, as you can see.

(CHARLES *moves above the table* C)

HENRIETTA. Well, that's a relief, for all our sakes. If you got better it would only make Father worse.
ARABEL. Henrietta!
HENRIETTA (*flinging herself at Elizabeth; all contrition*) Darling, darling, I didn't mean it! (*She kneels upstage on the sofa*) Nothing in the whole world matters to me, if only you're well. You know that, don't you?

(ARABEL *moves down* R *and puts paper in the rack on the desk*)

ELIZABETH. Yes, of course I do. But what you said about Father is quite untrue.
HENRIETTA (*rising and joining Septimus at the window*) I'm sorry. It's just that he's in one of his moods . . .
SEPTIMUS. And whose fault's that?

(HENRIETTA *takes two sweets from* SEPTIMUS, *eats one and throws the other to Alfred as she moves down* R *of the sofa*)

ARABEL (*to Henrietta*) Yes, why *can't* you realize that if there's one thing Papa will never, *never* permit, it's a romance in the family?
HENRIETTA (*defiantly*) If he had a penny, I'd run away with him tomorrow!

(ARABEL *swoons*)

ALFRED. Oh Lord, she's off again.

(HENRY *helps Arabel onto the chair at the desk.* ALFRED *and* CHARLES *move to her*)

CHARLES. Smelling salts!

GEORGE (*throwing over the smelling salts from the table in the alcove*) Smelling salts! (*He sits in the chair in the alcove up* LC)

ELIZABETH. Run away? With whom?

HENRIETTA (*sitting* L *of the table* C) Surtees, of course.

OCTAVIUS. You wouldn't d-d-d-d-dare.

HENRIETTA. Oh, w-w-w-w-wouldn't I?

GEORGE. Surtees. Now there's a name.

HENRIETTA. What's wrong with it?

CHARLES. "Surtees Cook, with the military look—"

HENRY (*moving down* L "—Added Henrietta to his little black book."

HENRIETTA (*rising*) You beast! (*She chases Henry down* L *and hurls herself at him*)

(*A friendly brawl develops, involving all the* BROTHERS. ELIZABETH *lies back, laughing happily.* ALFRED *follows Henrietta and smacks her.* HENRIETTA *turns and chases Alfred round the table* C. ARABEL *rises to stop them. They are stopped by a peremptory thumping from the ceiling overhead. The fight stops instantly.* ARABEL *sits* L *of the table* C, ALFRED *in the desk chair.* GEORGE *is up* R, CHARLES *up* RC, HENRIETTA *up* LC, OCTAVIUS *above the sofa,* SEPTIMUS *at the head of the sofa,* HENRY *down* L. ALL *look up*)

GEORGE (*speaking in Barrett's voice*) Your know your sister must avoid excitement.

CHARLES (*doing the same*) Especially before she retires for the night.

SEPTIMUS (*doing the same*) Absolute quiet essential in the sick room.

OCTAVIUS (*doing the same*) I am g-gravely displeased.

GEORGE (*nervously*) Yes, well, we'd better go before he comes down.

CHARLES. Why? You're not afraid of him, are you?

GEORGE. Yes, and so are you.

OCTAVIUS. I'm not.

SEPTIMUS. No?

OCTAVIUS. No, I'm absolutely p-petrified.

ALL. Good night, Ba. Good night, dear. 'Night, old thing. Sleep well, etc.

(*The* BROTHERS, *except* SEPTIMUS, *exit.* SEPTIMUS *brings the writing desk from the alcove and puts it on the table below the sofa. He then moves to the door, arriving there just in time to catch Arabel when she faints at the end of the following passage of dialogue*)

ARABEL (*to Henrietta*) You didn't really mean that—about running away?
HENRIETTA. I'd elope with him tonight, if I could!
ARABEL (*faintly*) Elope! Oh, mercy!

(ARABEL *faints through the doorway.* SEPTIMUS *catches her, and they exit.* HENRIETTA *moves up to follow them, turning out the gas bracket by the door*)

ELIZABETH. Henrietta—bring him to see me—one day when Papa is out.
HENRIETTA (*kneeling above the sofa*) Oh, I do love you! (*She hugs Elizabeth*)
ELIZABETH. And him?
HENRIETTA. Yes—oh yes, poor darling!
ELIZABETH. If he has your love, he's rich, my dear.
HENRIETTA. But he hasn't a penny. (*Rising and moving to the door*) None of us has—except you.
ELIZABETH (*with a flash of bitterness*) What use is money when one's locked in a cage and can't get out?

"THE WORLD OUTSIDE"

No. 5

The curtain is olive green
The quilt on the bed is red
The carpet's hue is the gentle blue
Of the ceiling over my head

(HENRIETTA *sits on the sofa and takes Elizabeth's hand*)

This is the world I know is safe
Why do I long instead
For the world I dread?

Nothing as blue as sky is
Nothing as gentle as July is
Whispering sounds of Summer to
The World outside
Nothing as fair as dawn is
Nothing as yellow-tipped as corn is
Glittering in the golden
Countryside
I have my own quiet room
My very special private place
But, oh, to know the sun again
And feel its glow upon my face
Gone all my fears
Gone every haunting shadow
Gone forever
Nothing as soft as Spring is
Nothing as green as each green thing is
Roses appear and crocuses cheer with pride

In my longed-for wonderful
World outside.
HENRIETTA (*rising to* c) But, Ba, think what you're missing.
ELIZABETH. I am.
HENRIETTA. No, I mean the bad things. (*Singing*)
Nothing as grey as clouds are
ELIZABETH (*singing*)
Nothing as gay as London crowds are
Wandering by my window in
The World outside
HENRIETTA (*moving to Elizabeth and taking her hand*)
Nothing as cold as night is
ELIZABETH.
Nothing so touched with true delight is
Scattering moon and stardust—

(HENRIETTA *moves* c *and sits* L *of the table*)

Far and wide
HENRIETTA.
You have your own peaceful room
And every tender loving care
ELIZABETH.
But, oh, if I could leave it all
And breathe the free, fresh open air
Free like a bird
Free not to fear tomorrow
Ah, tomorrow
Nothing as cool as streams are
Nothing as foolish as my dreams are
Longing to see, but ever to be denied
That, oh, so magically marvellous
Great big boundlessly beautiful
Whole wide wonderful World outside!

HENRIETTA (*rising and sitting on the end of the sofa*) I never knew
you felt like that. You always seem so placid and resigned.
ELIZABETH. Yes, well, there's one thing I'm not resigned to—
and that's porter. (*Grimacing, she picks up the tankard of beer again*)
HENRIETTA. Leave it. (*She rises and takes the tankard*)
ELIZABETH. No. Papa will notice and there'll be a scene.
HENRIETTA. No, there won't. (*She goes to the desk and pours the
porter into a pot on it*)
ELIZABETH. Henrietta! You'll kill the azalea!
HENRIETTA. Better it than you.

(BARRETT *enters up* RC, *unseen by* HENRIETTA)

It needed water anyw . . . (*She stops dead as she sees Barrett in
the doorway*)

(*There is a terrible silence*)

Barrett (*at length*) Go down to the kitchen and fetch another tankard of porter immediately.

Henrietta. No.

Barrett. I beg your pardon?

Henrietta (*running above the sofa and taking Elizabeth's hand; her voice trembling with anger and agitation*) It's—it's sheer cruelty. You know how Ba hates the stuff. You're just torturing her because—because you like torturing.

Barrett. I have told you to fetch a tankard of porter.

Henrietta. I won't do it.

Barrett. Obey me this instant!

Elizabeth. Go and fetch it, Henrietta! I can't stand this . . .

Henrietta. But, Ba, you know how you . . .

Elizabeth. Please—please . . .

(*After a moment's indecision* Henrietta *turns and exits.* Barrett *moves above the sofa*)

It was my fault. She did it for me. She knows I detest it.

Barrett. Porter has invaluable blood-making properties.

Elizabeth. Yes, I know, but I hate it, Papa. Surely something one abominates can't do one any good.

Barrett. Forgive me if I point out that you are not necessarily the best judge of what is good or bad for you. (*The opened letter catches his eye*) Your usual letter?

Elizabeth. Yes, Papa.

Barrett. From the versifier Browning?

Elizabeth. Mr Robert Browning, the poet, yes.

Barrett. An importunate correspondent.

Elizabeth. He admires my work and asks to call. He has written a play for Mr Macready.

Barrett. Indeed.

Elizabeth. It's to be given at the Haymarket Theatre.

Barrett. Indeed.

Elizabeth. He has great hopes for it.

Barrett. Indeed. When he first communicated with you some months ago, you mentioned, if memory serves, that you had declined to see him.

Elizabeth. Yes.

Barrett. Shall you do so again?

Elizabeth. Yes, Papa.

Barrett. A wise decision.

Elizabeth. When people admire my work they incline to picture the poetess as beautiful as her verses. It's humiliating to disillusion them.

Barrett. You're very interesting and picturesque, my dear.

Elizabeth. Isn't that how guide-books describe a ruin?

(Henrietta *enters with a tankard of porter*)

Give it to me, please.

(HENRIETTA *moves towards Elizabeth, but* BARRETT *stops her*)

BARRETT. No. (*He takes the tankard. To Henrietta*) You may go.
HENRIETTA. Good night, Ba, darling . . .
BARRETT (*sharply*) You may go.

(HENRIETTA *exits*)

ELIZABETH. Please give me the tankard.

BARRETT (*moving above the sofa to the window and putting the tankard on the dresser; with a complete change of manner*) Let's forget the porter for tonight, shall we? If you and I are to have a difference of opinion, let it at least be over something substantial. But *we* must never quarrel, Elizabeth—(*bringing the chair from the alcove to* R *of the sofa and sitting*)—and especially not last thing at night. This is our time, isn't it? When I come to your room at the end of the day—and we sit here quietly—just the two of us—and talk. I wonder if you have any conception with what eagerness I look forward to these quiet moments alone with you. For me this room holds all I know of peace and comfort, of happiness and love. You are very dear and precious to me, Elizabeth. You know that. Without you I should be quite alone. I thank God for you, my child. (*He rises and puts the chair back in the alcove*)

(ELIZABETH *puts her hand to her eyes to hide her emotions*)

You're not feeling worse tonight, my darling?
ELIZABETH. No, Papa.
BARRETT. Just tired?
ELIZABETH. Just tired.
BARRETT. You must rest. (*He kneels upstage of the sofa*) Almighty and most merciful God, in thine inscrutable wisdom Thou hast seen good to lay on Thy daughter Elizabeth grievous and heavy afflictions. For years she has languished in sickness. Fill her with the spirit of resignation and acceptance. Give her to understand the blessed word that Thou chastiseth those whom Thou lovest. Guard and comfort her through all her days. Amen.
ELIZABETH. Amen.
BARRETT (*rising*) Good night, my dearest child.
ELIZABETH. Good night, Papa.

BARRETT *goes to the dresser, takes the tankard, and sets it unobtrusively on the table below the sofa. He then moves to the desk, turns out the lamp on it, and exits* R. ELIZABETH *looks after him, then at the tankard. She picks it up, is about to drink, then puts it down decisively. She picks up the letter and her writing desk, and is about to start writing a letter as the* LIGHTS *fade.*

SCENE CHANGE MUSIC   No.
                                      8

SCENE 4

The open stage of the Theatre Royal, Haymarket

As the LIGHTS *come up, the scene is a bedlam of activity and confusion before a dress rehearsal of the play "King Victor and Prince Charles" by Robert Browning, which the Macready Company plan to present. To a musical accompaniment we see* STAGE HANDS *moving tables and props under the direction of a* STAGE MANAGER, SCENE PAINTERS *on a platform painting a back-cloth, two* ACTORS *rehearsing a duel, two other* ACTORS *(a man and a woman) quarrelling, a* BARMAID *with tankards of beer, a* CHARWOMAN *cleaning the floor, etc. Weaving a way slowly through the bedlam comes* EVANS, *Browning's manservant, a cheerful cockney, with a letter in his hat. Fascinated by the backstage scene and getting in everyone's way,* EVANS *eventually sinks onto a skip or laundry-basket* RC, *from which he watches the proceedings, goggle-eyed. The Great Man himself,* WILLIAM MACREADY, *enters up* L, *in full costume for his role. The atmosphere, which is vulgar, Hogarthian and seething with life, is in total contrast to the secluded refinement of Wimpole Street.* MACREADY *moves down* C, *holding his script.*

MACREADY (*shouting to the Orchestra*) A little less noise, please, from the pit!

(*The music stops*)

Thank you. (*To the Stage Manager*) Mr Langton!
LANGTON. Yes, Mr Macready, sir! (*He takes the script from Macready*)
MACREADY. Ladies and gentlemen, may I have your close attention for a few minor details. (*To the Charwoman at his feet*) Not now, dear—after the rehearsal.

(*The* CHARWOMAN *moves upstage*)

Perruquier!

(*A* PERRUQUIER *helps* MACREADY *on with his wig*)

Take it again, Mr Harrison, from "Well . . ."—from "Well . . ."
LANGTON. From "Well, Savoy turns Sardinia, the Duke's King."
MACREADY. Thank you. And would it ho possible to have a brief quietus?
LANGTON (*to the Company*) Quiet, please!
MACREADY. Don't rush it, Mr Harrison, take your time. The play I grant is bad, but thank God, short.
LANGTON. Positions, please.

(*One of the actors,* HARRISON, *moves down* R; *the actress,* MRS BUTLER, *moves* L *of Harrison. Another actor,* HOWARD, *moves close to Macready on his* L, *carrying a crown on a cushion.* LANGTON *stands down* L)

MACREADY (*to Howard*) Down, sir, don't crowd the stage. Open it out.

(HOWARD *moves away* L)

HARRISON (*who plays "Charles"*) "Well, Savoy turns Sardinia ..."

(LANGTON *thrusts through the players to supervise the* STAGE HANDS, *who start setting a throne* C)

MACREADY. Mr Langton, I am endeavouring to rehearse this deplorable piece . . .

LANGTON (*moving* R *of Macready*) Yes, sir, Mr Macready, but you want a performance tonight, sir, don't you?

MACREADY. I do not *want* it, Mr Langton. I am resigned to it.

LANGTON. Thank you, Mr Macready, sir.

(*When the throne is in place,* LANGTON *moves down* L)

MACREADY (*sitting on the throne; with a martyred air*) Once more, Mr Harrison, those immortal lines . . .

HARRISON. "Well, Savoy turns Sardinia. The Duke's king . . ."

MRS BUTLER. "Endure, endure, Beloved! Say you not he is your father?"

MACREADY. Splendid, dear. (*Rising and speaking as "Victor", in measured tones, taking his time with the pauses*) "My son, obey me!—

(HARRISON *moves* R *of Macready and kneels to him*)

                                        —Charles,
            Your father, clearer-sighted than yourself
            Decides it must be so."

(MACREADY *turns to Howard to receive the crown.* HOWARD *gives the crown to Macready, but is a little late on cue*)

HOWARD (*who plays "D'Ormea"*) "Sir, for the last time, pause!"

(MACREADY *pauses. He gives the pause, as is his wont, its full weight. So much so that a disembodied voice from the back of the auditorium cries out in an agony of expectation*)

VOICE. Well, go on, man, go *on*! We haven't got all night!

(ROBERT BROWNING, *whose voice it is, enters from the auditorium to down* L. *There is a sudden hush from those on stage. Outraged,* MACREADY *looks about him*)

MACREADY. I *beg* your pardon? (*He gives the crown to Howard*)

(HOWARD *puts the crown on the table* L. HARRISON *rises*)

BROWNING. And so you should, by Heaven, if that's the way you mean to play the King.

MACREADY (*roaring*) Mr Langton, for the last time, *EJECT THAT MAN!*

BROWNING (*moving to* R *of Langton*) You can't eject the author, sir.

(BROWNING, *who now comes into full view, is immaculately dressed in high hat and morning coat, and carries a clouded cane and lemon-coloured gloves*)

My contract stipulates the author shall be entitled to attend rehearsals. Am I or am I not the author of "King Victor and King Charles"? (*He takes the script from Langton*)

(LANGTON *moves upstage*)

MACREADY. Mr Browning, you are—and, sir, you have my deepest sympathy.

BROWNING. If that was a sample of your performance, sir, I shall need it. In the name of Melpomene, what were you waiting for—Armageddon?

MACREADY (*heavily*) Your execrable text said "Pause"—I paused.

BROWNING (*moving to* R *of Macready*) You pause as long as that, Macready, Monday's audience will still be here when Tuesday's arrives.

MACREADY. With your play, sir, there will be no audience on Tuesday. You may be a major poet, Mr Browning, you cannot write a play for the theatre.

BROWNING. What is wrong with my play, sir?

MACREADY. When I have a month to spare I will tell you, sir. (*He turns away* L)

BROWNING. There's nothing wrong with the piece if you'd only get on with it. Those yawning gulfs of yours would murder Othello!

MACREADY (*turning to Browning*) Permit me to inform you, Mr Browning, you are not *yet* William Shakespeare.

BROWNING. And allow me to inform you, sir, you never *will* be David Garrick or Edmund Kean!

MACREADY (*taking off his wig and throwing it to the Perruquier*) I, sir, am William Charles Macready—and that, sir, is enough for most men!

BROWNING (*aside*) Yes, and for some too much!

MACREADY. I heard that, sir!

BROWNING (*turning*) You were meant to, sir!

MACREADY (*livid*) Mr Langton—

(LANGTON *moves* R *of Macready*)

—in one hour we dress rehearse, God help us! Dismiss this unhappy consortium of players!

(MACREADY *storms off the stage*)

LANGTON. Right, clear everyone! Clear, please! Dress rehearsal four-thirty! Clear the stage!

(*The* COMPANY *and* STAGE STAFF, *who have been fascinated by the row between Star and Author, exit reluctantly, removing tables and props as they go.* Two STAGE HANDS *take the throne off up* R. LANGTON *follows.* EVANS *and* BROWNING *are left alone, except for a* SCENE PAINTER *who continues working upstage.* BROWNING *moves up* R, *looking at his watch.* EVANS *moves* L *of him*)

EVANS. Drop o' beer, sir?

BROWNING (*surprised*) What? Hello, Evans, where did you spring from?

EVANS. Home, sir. I brought the letter, sir. (*Rapt*) I never been backstage before, sir. Gorgeous, isn't it?

BROWNING. Sublime!

EVANS (*wandering about the stage*) It's like a wonderland. (*He sniffs*) Got its own smell, too. Sort of a mixture of—of magic and—er . . .

BROWNING. Sweat.

EVANS. That's it exactly, sir. Sweat and magic. Magic and sweat. (*He moves* C)

BROWNING (*moving down* L) What brings you here?

EVANS. This letter, sir. The lady's maid brought it. Very Wimpole Street, she was.

BROWNING (*suddenly galvanized*) Wimpole Street! It must be from her! Let's have it, let's have it. (*He moves to* L *of Evans*)

EVANS. Sir?

BROWNING. The letter, man, the letter!

EVANS. Right here, sir. I—now that's a funny thing—where did I . . . (*He looks about him blankly*)

BROWNING. Evans, I warn you, if you've lost that letter . . .

EVANS (*feeling in his pockets*) Not lost, sir, not lost. Just mislaid. I—I'll find it, sir . . .

BROWNING (*crossing above Evans to* R *of him*) You'd better, and fast, or . . . (*He sees the letter in Evans's hat*) Evans, you're wearing it. (*He snatches the letter and tears it open*)

EVANS. Bad news, sir?

BROWNING (*gradually*) Bad news? You've just brought me the most superlatively *good* news since the dove brought the first green leaf to Noah!

EVANS. Why? What's happened, Mr Browning, sir?

BROWNING (*dramatically*) She's invited me to tea.

EVANS (*flatly*) Oh, that's nice.

BROWNING. Nice? Man, the heavens have opened!

"THE MOON IN MY POCKET"   No. 9

(*singing*)
Tell the sky—

(EVANS *moves to the table down* L. *The* SCENE PAINTER *comes down his ladder onto the stage. The rest of the* COMPANY, *with the exception of* MACREADY, *gradually enter*)

I carry the moon in my pocket
Down came the moon like a rocket
And plummeted into my pocket
The morning sun
Must have forgotten to lock it
Now I carry the moon in my pocket
And the lining is shining with stars
Depressed was I
When suddenly out of the blue came
Glittering, crescent and new came
A luminous letter from you came
Now hope soars high
And nothing can possibly stop it
I carry the moon in my pocket
And my jacket is Venus and Mars
Trumpets, ring out!
Come, choristers, sing out!
Every bold bright banner and flag be unfurled!
The moon and I
Are treading a heavenly highway
Anyone travelling my way?
All's right with the world!
I carry the moon, a magical moon
A marvellous moon in my pocket
A magical moon, a mellifluous tune
And all's right with the world

ENSEMBLE.
You carry the moon
A magical moon
A marvellous moon in your pocket
A magical moon, a catch of a tune
And all's right with the world!

BROWNING.	ENSEMBLE.
(*singing, together*)	
Tell the planets	Tell the sky
Tell the stars	You carry the moon in your pocket
Tell whoever	Down came the moon like a rocket
Lives on Mars	And plummeted into your pocket

The thrilling tale
Has just arrived
Just
   arrived
By special
   mail

The morning sun
Must have forgotten to lock it
Now you carry the
   moon in your pocket
And the lining is shining
   with stars

BROWNING *and* ENSEMBLE (*together*)
   Lightning, thunder!
   The earth is a wonder

BROWNING.
   See where every valley and hill is dew-pearled

BROWNING *and* ENSEMBLE (*together*)
   The milky way
   Has added a carpet of glory
   And the finishing touch to the story
   Is all's right with the world

BROWNING.
   The finishing touch
   The delicate touch
   The twist in the wrist of the story

BROWNING *and* ENSEMBLE (*together*)
   The ultimate touch
   Is certainly such
   That all's right with the world.

BROWNING.   ENSEMBLE.

(*singing together*)

Tell the planets
Tell the
   stars
Tell who-
   ever
Lives on
   Mars
The thrilling tale
Has just arrived
Just
   arrived
By special
   mail

Tell the sky
You carry the moon in your
   pocket
Down came the moon like a
   rocket
And plummeted into your
   pocket
The morning sun
Must have forgotten to lock it
Now you carry the
   moon in your pocket
And the lining is shining
   stars

BROWNING *and* ENSEMBLE (*together*)
   Trumpets, ring out!
   Come, choristers, sing out!
   Every bold bright banner and flag be unfurled!
   The moon and I
   Are treading a heavenly highway
   Anyone travelling my way?
   All's right with the world!

BROWNING.
    The moon is as light
    The moon is as light
    The moon is as light as a feather
    It comes from above
    And when you're in love
    All's right with the world!
BROWNING *and* ENSEMBLE (*together*)
    Band, crescendo!
    Come, orchestra, blend! Oh,
    Let your clear imperious message be hurled!
    Proclaim to all
    The moon is as light as a feather
    If you and your love are together
    All's right, all's right, all's right with the world!
    (BROWNING *and the* COMPANY *retire upstage and exit up* R *and up* L *as the* LIGHTS *fade*)
    All's right with the world!
    All's right with the world!

SCENE CHANGE MUSIC   No.
10

SCENE 5
Elizabeth's room

When the LIGHTS *come up,* ELIZABETH, *dressed, is lying on her sofa, nervously checking the tea-tray which* WILSON *has just placed on the table below it.*

WILSON (*moving to the table* C) I'll bring the teapot as soon as he comes, miss.

ELIZABETH (*clattering cutlery*) Cake knife. I don't see the cake knife.

WILSON (*moving up* R *to tidy the books; patiently*) Beside the plate, miss.

ELIZABETH. Oh, yes. Spoons. I only see one sp—Oh! (*In her nervousness she knocks the spoons on the floor*)

WILSON (*moving above the sofa*) Are you feeling all right, miss? (*She moves down* L *to pick up the spoons and replace them*)

ELIZABETH. No—that is, yes, I . . .

    (*There is a knock on the door up* RC)

(*Panicked*) He's here!

    (HENRIETTA *bursts in to above the sofa*)

HENRIETTA (*in great excitement*) Ba, you must see him at once! You positively must! He's in his full Regimentals.

ELIZABETH (*bewildered*) What?

HENRIETTA. He's just been to the Palace to receive his adjutancy or something from the Queen herself, and—oh, he's wonderful, he's gorgeous.

ELIZABETH. Who is?

HENERITTA. Surtees, of course. He's outside on the landing. (*Moving to the door*) May he come in?

ELIZABETH. No, dear, I'm expecting a visitor. Some other time. Wilson, is there enough milk?

HENRIETTA. Ba! You promised to meet him when Father was out, and I smuggled him in the back way specially.

ELIZABETH (*resigned*) Wilson, ask the gentleman on the landing to come in, please.

WILSON. Very good, miss.

(WILSON *moves below the sofa to the door.* HENRIETTA *moves above the sofa.* WILSON *holds the door open for* SURTEES COOK *to enter, then exits, shutting it.* COOK *moves* C. *He is in the full splendour of his "Regimentals", his breastplate gleaming, his helmet under one arm.* COOK *is a simple, diffident and good-hearted soul*)

HENRIETTA. Captain Surtees Cook, Ba. My sister, Elizabeth.

(COOK *clicks his heels together and bows*)

COOK. Your servant, Miss Barrett.

ELIZABETH (*offering him her hand*) How do you do?

COOK (*taking Elizabeth's hand and bowing over it*) Greatly honoured, 'pon my word, Miss Barrett. Understand not every-one received here.

HENRIETTA. No. Very few gentlemen have ever been allowed in Ba's room.

COOK. I should hope not—that is—absolutely.

HENRIETTA. Ba, isn't he beautiful?

COOK. Oh, I say . . .

ELIZABETH. Yes, indeed, Captain, you look quite magnificent.

COOK. Do I? (*He considers the point*) Yes, I suppose I do. (*He beams*)

HENRIETTA (*taking Cook's helmet and putting it on the chair in the alcove*) Go on, tell her.

COOK. What?

HENRIETTA. You know . . .

COOK. Oh! Ah! Yes, b'Jove. Er—Miss Barrett . . .

ELIZABETH. Yes?

COOK. Miss Barrett . . .

ELIZABETH. Captain Cook?

COOK. What? I say, Miss Barrett—er . . .

ELIZABETH. You want to tell me something about Henrietta, Captain Cook?

COOK. Just so, Miss Barrett. Just so. That is—in other words —exactly. Never was such a girl, y'know—Henrietta, I mean. Fact is—well . . .

HENRIETTA. Oh, for Heaven's sake! Ba, Surtees has just asked me to marry him!

ELIZABETH. Marry!

HENRIETTA (*moving to the chair* L *of the table* C *and sitting*) And, of course, I accepted him and said that I couldn't. Ba, what *are* we to do? We love each other terribly . . .
COOK. I say—steady!
HENRIETTA. And Surtees has only just enough money to keep himself decently and . . .
COOK. More than willing to throw up soldiering and take to some moneymaking business.
HENRIETTA. Ba, can *you* make him understand? About Papa, I mean. I can't.
ELIZABETH. Captain Cook, I realize how you feel about Henrietta, but if you were a Prince of Eldorado, with a pedigree from some signory in the moon in one hand and a ticket of good behaviour from the nearest Independent Chapel in the other— even then my father would show you the door. *Now* do you understand?
COOK (*after a moment's thought*) No, I can't say that I do.
ELIZABETH. To put it simply—nothing at all in this house must happen without my father's sanction.
COOK. Oh, I see. Oh! I say!
HENRIETTA. He once owned slaves in Jamaica. Now *we're* his slaves.
ELIZABETH. Henrietta! In his own way he loves us all.
HENRIETTA. Love? When we have to obey his every whim? That's not what I call love. Oh, Ba, if only I had your four-hundred a year . . .
ELIZABETH. My dear, I'd give it to you—and how gladly . . .
HENRIETTA. I know you would, darling, but that's utterly impossible.
COOK. Jove, yes. Can't live off a woman. There's a word for that. I don't know what it is but there's a word for it.
HENRIETTA (*rising and moving above the sofa*) It's not that. Just think what Ba's life would be like if Papa knew she'd made it possible for me to marry.
COOK (*moving to the bookcase up* R) Must say he sounds an extraordinary feller . . .

(*There is a knock at the door*)

ELIZABETH. This must be my visitor. Captain Cook, it's been a pleasure . . .

(BELLA HEDLEY *enters, followed by* HENRY BEVAN. BELLA *moves up* LC. BEVAN *closes the door.* HENRIETTA *moves down* L)

BELLA. Surpwise, surpwise! Surpwise, surpwise!
ELIZABETH (*not overjoyed*) Oh, it's you, Bella.
BELLA. I know we're not expected, and I do hope it's not too fwantically wude, but Hawy and I just happened to be passing and I said to Hawy, "I simply must intwoduce my fiancé to my

famous cousin". Deawest Ba, this is my Hawy. Hawy—Miss
Elizabeth Bawwett.
BEVAN (*bowing*) An honour, Miss Barrett.
ELIZABETH (*offering her hand*) I hope you'll both be vewy—
er—very happy.
BEVAN. I won't come too close.
BELLA. Hawy hates sickwooms. He's a hypochondwiac.
ELIZABETH. I'm not infectious, you know.
BEVAN. Better to be safe than—er . . .
BELLA. Sowwy, Hawy.
BEVAN. For what, my love? Ah! Confusion, confusion.

(COOK *moves down* R. BELLA *sits on the* R *end of the sofa*)

BELLA. Deawest Ba, so spiwitual, so near to Heaven. You have
a look in your eyes, darling, as though you aleady saw the
angels.
HENRIETTA. She's looking at me, Bella—and I'm no angel.
BELLA. No, I'm afwaid you're not, Henwietta, but . . . (*She
suddenly sees Cook*) Oh! Who is this gorgeous cweature? (*She
rises and moves* L *of Cook*)
HENRIETTA. Captain Cook is Alfred and Occy's friend.
BELLA (*slyly*) And yours?
HENRIETTA (*defiantly*) And mine!
BELLA. I thought so! How thwilling!

(COOK *clicks his heels and bows*)

Oh, how militawy! Henwietta darling, you must come to the
wedding and be one of my bwidesmaids. (*To Cook*) And so
must you.
COOK. I say . . .
BELLA (*sitting on the chair* L *of the table* C) And so must Awabel.
Henwietta, you will, won't you?
HENRIETTA (*moving above the sofa*) Of course I will—if Papa—
no, I don't see how he could possibly object.
BELLA. Object? *Darling*, you're only asked to be a bwides-
maid, not a bwide!

(WILSON *enters*)

WILSON (*crossing down* L *to adjust the window curtains; with
suppressed excitement*) He's here, miss. I showed him into the
library.
BELLA. Who is here?
HENRIETTA. Never mind.
BELLA. I'm just dying of cuwiosity. Awen't I dweadful?
HENRIETTA (*moving upstage of Bella*) Yes, you are! I'll see you
out.
BELLA (*rising and moving above the sofa*) Au wevoir, deawest
Ba. (*She kisses Elizabeth*)

ELIZABETH. Good-bye, Bella.
BELLA. So fwail, so etheweal, so fwagile and pwactically in Pawadise. *A wiverderci.* Come along, Hawy.

(BELLA *exits.* BEVAN *bows and follows her.* ELIZABETH *coughs to attract* COOK's *attention, but he is absorbed in contemplating Henrietta*)

ELIZABETH (*at length*) Good-bye, Captain.
COOK (*crossing to shake hands with Elizabeth*) Oh! Are you leaving?
WILSON (*moving to the alcove*) No, sir, you are. (*She hands Cook his helmet*)
COOK. What? Oh, yes! So I am. By Jove!

(HENRIETTA *exits, followed by* COOK)

WILSON (*moving to the door*) Now, miss?
ELIZABETH (*her panic returning*) No, Wilson. No, I can't see him. I don't feel up to it.
WILSON (*moving to the sofa*) Miss, what on earth is the matter?
ELIZABETH. Say I'm very sorry, but I'm not well enough to receive him.
WILSON (*severely*) But that's not true, miss.
ELIZABETH (*with a rueful grin*) No, it's not true.

(WILSON *moves to the door*)

Wilson . . .?
WILSON. Yes, miss?
ELIZABETH. Is—is my hair tidy?

(WILSON *moves to the sofa for a quick look at Elizabeth's hair*)

WILSON (*returning to the door*) Lovely, dear—lovely.
ELIZABETH. And my—please arrange the covers.

(WILSON *returns to arrange the covers and returns to the door*)

Oh, and Wilson, my fan.

(WILSON *takes the fan from the table* C *and gives it to Elizabeth*)

WILSON (*at length*) Now, miss?

(ELIZABETH *takes a deep breath*)

ELIZABETH. Now.

(WILSON *exits, leaving the door open.* ELIZABETH *clasps her hands to steady them, sees them tremble again, starts to panic in earnest, and reaches for a bottle of pills on the bedside table. Unseen,* BROWNING *appears in the doorway.* ELIZABETH *opens the bottle of pills and shakes two into her shaking palm*)

BROWNING (*moving down from the doorway; softly*) Miss Barrett . . .?

ELIZABETH (*with a violent start*) Oh! (*The jerk of her hands shoots the entire contents of the bottle into the room. Pills fly in all directions, half of them hitting Browning*) Oh, forgive me, I—how stupid and clumsy . . .

BROWNING. My fault entirely for approaching so quietly—not normally a failing of mine.

ELIZABETH. No, no it was my . . . (*She dabs ineffectively at the pills in the immediate area of the sofa*)

BROWNING. Allow me. (*He puts his gloves and a book on the table* C, *then goes on hands and knees below the sofa to pick up pills*)

ELIZABETH. Please, Mr Browning, your beautiful suit . . .

BROWNING. A test of good cloth. If it fails to survive I shall change my tailor. You know, Miss Barrett, I pictured our first meeting a thousand ways, but I never imagined this delightful variant of hunt the slipper. Excuse me. (*He dives under the sofa*)

ELIZABETH. Please get up, Mr Browning. I'm acutely embarrassed.

BROWNING. Quite unnecessary, I assure you. I'm enjoying myself enormously.

ELIZABETH. I—I can't possibly have Mr Robert Browning sprawled at my feet!

BROWNING. My dear Miss Barrett, he's been there for months. (*He rises above the sofa with several pills and hands them to Elizabeth*) What are they for?

ELIZABETH (*fanning herself feverishly*) A—a sedative for the nerves.

BROWNING. And the prospect of meeting Robert Browning sent you straight to the bottle?

ELIZABETH. No, no . . .

BROWNING. A wise precaution. Forgive me again. (*He crosses to the desk down* R *to pick up more pills*)

ELIZABETH. Mr Browning!

BROWNING (*gaily, half-hidden under the desk*) A few more under here, Miss Barrett.

(WILSON *enters with the teapot and moves down* C. *She sees the figure of the prostrate poet and stands rooted, letting the tea spill from the pot*)

ELIZABETH (*dismissing her*) Thank you, Wilson.

(WILSON *is transfixed*)

Wilson!

(WILSON *moves below the sofa, puts the teapot on the tray, then exits, reluctantly*)

BROWNING (*rising, moving above the sofa, and handing the pills to Elizabeth*) There.

ELIZABETH (*with relief*) Thank you for—for so gallantly coming to my rescue.

Browning. The herald of things to come, Miss Barrett. (*Offering a pill*) Would you care for one now?

Elizabeth. No, thank you. I'm entirely composed.

Browning. You're quite sure?

Elizabeth. Quite sure. Won't you sit down? (*She pours tea*)

Browning (*moving* c) Extraordinary. This room, I mean. You may think this is the first time I've been here. You're quite wrong. I know every inch of it.

Elizabeth. But that's impossible . . .

Browning (*moving* R *to the desk*) From your cousin, Mr Kenyon.

Elizabeth. Mr Kenyon has been talking to you about me?

Browning. Oh, no. There was nothing he could tell me about you personally which has the slightest interest for me.

Elizabeth. Really. Your tea.

Browning. You see, I knew all about you already—from your verses. (*He moves above the sofa*)

Elizabeth. Do they give me away so completely?

Browning (*taking his tea*) Thank you. Those poems are you, Miss Barrett.

Elizabeth (*with enthusiasm*) And yours are you. Those wonderful people of yours out of every age and country—they've trooped into this room and round this sofa. . . . Oh, you don't know what they've meant to me!

Browning. Do you really mean that?

Elizabeth. Yes, of course I . . .

Browning. Splendid. (*Briskly*) In that case, I'll come straight to the point.

Elizabeth. The point?

Browning. Of my visit. (*He goes to the table* c, *puts down his cup and picks up his gloves and book*) Miss Barrett, do you by any chance remember the first letter I wrote to you?

Elizabeth. Yes, Mr Browning, it was a wonderful letter.

Browning. You may have thought I dashed it off in a fit of white-hot enthusiasm over your poems. I didn't. I weighed every word of every sentence. (*He puts his gloves and book down again*) And of one sentence in particular: "I love your books with all my heart—and I love you too". You remember?

Elizabeth. Er—yes. I recall the sentence. (*She holds out a plate of teacakes*) A toasted teacake?

(Browning *moves above the sofa and takes a teacake*)

Browning. Thank you. (*He takes the chair from the alcove and sits upstage* R *of the sofa. Munching*) Where was I?

Elizabeth (*amused*) You love my books with all your heart and you love me, too. (*She puts the plate on the tray*)

Browning. Precisely. Miss Barrett, when you read those words, what was your reaction.

Elizabeth. Jam?

BROWNING. No jam.

ELIZABETH (*lightly*) Well now, let me see. Why, yes, I thought it charmingly impulsive of you.

BROWNING (*with a touch of irritation*) But I thought I had made it perfectly clear there was nothing impulsive about it.

ELIZABETH. Oh?

BROWNING. That sentence was as deeply felt and anxiously thought over as any sentence I have ever written.

ELIZABETH (*still keeping her tone deliberately light*) I hope I have many readers like you, Mr Browning. It's wonderful to think I may have good friends all the world over whom I have never seen.

BROWNING (*impatiently*) I am not speaking of friendship. I am speaking of love . . .

ELIZABETH. More tea?

"I SAID LOVE"

No.
II

(*Someone is heard practising the harmonium downstairs*)

BROWNING (*rising and moving* R) My dear Miss Barrett, it's quite useless your trying to put aside the word. I am neither mad nor morbidly impressionable; I am as sane and level-headed as any man living, and I tell you, in all soberness, you are the centre of my life.

ELIZABETH. I must apologize—my sister Arabel's practising . . .

BROWNING (*singing*)
> I said love and I mean love
> Let's be clear from the start
> Something very strange has happened
> Happened here in my heart
> Friendship can be quite delightful
> Having friends is very nice
> But, my dear friend, I must warn you
> Merely friendship won't suffice
> Now I'm rich, rich as Croesus
> Taller than St Peter's, Rome
> I've found where the golden fleece is
> Without even leaving home
> I said love and I mean love
> I repeat from the start
> Something very strange has happened
> Happened here in my heart

ELIZABETH (*spoken*) I really do apologize for the harmonium, it's my sister, Arabel . . .

BROWNING (*moving to replace the chair in the alcove; singing*)
> I said love and I mean love
> Now I know how it feels

Throwing bonnets over windmills
Going heart over heels—

(ELIZABETH *picks up the teapot, but* BROWNING *moves down* L *of the sofa and replaces it on the tray*)

This is love, you'll know it's love
When you've learnt what it can mean—

(ELIZABETH *picks up the teapot, but he takes it from her and puts it back again. She picks up the pillbox, and he takes that from her. She then picks up a glass of water*)

To be young when you're a hundred
To be old at seventeen,
This was planned, why dissemble?
Planned by fate, why pretend?

(BROWNING *moves above the sofa, takes the glass from her, and holds her hand*)

Take my hand, feel it tremble
Would it tremble for a friend?
I said love and I mean love
I repeat from the start
Something wonderful has happened
Happened here in my heart

ELIZABETH. I wonder if you'd be kind enough to give me that glass of water?

(BROWNING *gives her the glass*)

Thank you. (*She takes three pills rapidly one after the other and swallows them*)

(BROWNING *watches her, then moves* C, *takes one pill from the box and swallows it with tea from his cup which is on the table* C. *As he puts the cup down,* ELIZABETH *speaks*)

(*Gravely*) Mr Browning—

(BROWNING *puts the pillbox on the table then turns to her* C)

—if I were to take you seriously it would, of course, mean the immediate end of a pleasant friendship.
BROWNING. Why?
ELIZABETH. You must know that love—in the sense that you apparently use the word—has, and can have, no place in my life.
BROWNING (*sitting on the pouffe downstage and facing her*) Why?
ELIZABETH. For many reasons—but one will suffice. I am a dying woman.
BROWNING. Rubbish! Forgive me, but you must never say such a thing again. I forbid it!
ELIZABETH. Forbid . . .?

Browning. Yes, forbid. For if what you say were remotely conceivable, God would be callous, and I know he's compassionate—and life would be evil and I know it's good. That, I trust, disposes of that.

Elizabeth (*fascinated*) When you speak like that, you sound so very much like Edward.

Browning. Edward?

Elizabeth. My eldest brother. He died—some years ago. We were on holiday—in Torquay—when—he was drowned.

Browning. I'm deeply sorry.

Elizabeth. We were very close. I—he had stopped behind an extra week on my account—at my request. But for me—he would not have been there that day.

Browning (*watching her; shrewdly*) And you blame yourself for your brother's death?

Elizabeth (*swiftly*) Why should I?

Browning (*rising and moving up* R) And since then you decided to shut yourself up in these four walls in dust, dimness and staleness of air and join him as promptly as possible?

Elizabeth (*quickly, defensively*) I—I decided nothing. I'm a sick woman.

Browning (*bluntly*) Miss Barrett, what are you dying of? Apart, that is, from lack of oxygen.

Elizabeth (*with rising anger*) I'm sorry if the room is uncomfortably warm. My doctor insists on a hothouse temperature.

Browning (*sitting* L *of the table* C; *irrepressibly*) The right diagnosis, the wrong prescription! The warmth you need is the heat of the sun—the Mediterranean—Italy. Italy! Now, there's a country. Warm beaches, beauty, the sense of the past. We must go there together as soon as you're well. (*He rises*)

Elizabeth. You seem to forget I am unable to put one foot in front of the other.

Browning. I don't accept that for one moment—and neither must you.

Elizabeth (*recovering her equanimity*) What nonsense—what delightful nonsense you talk, Mr Browning.

Browning (*moving up* R *of the sofa; urgently*) Miss Barrett, don't you *want* to be well?

Elizabeth. *Want?* You think it's a question of wanting?

Browning. In your case—yes! A thousand times, yes!

"WANT TO BE WELL"

No.
12

(*singing*)   Want to be well
That is the way
Say that you will
And you may

Want to be well—

(ELIZABETH *turns away from him*)

There is the plan
Know that you will
And you can

(BROWNING *moves above the sofa to down* L *as Elizabeth sings,
then crosses downstage to down* R)

ELIZABETH (*singing*)
Do you think it's as simple as that?
Do you think at the drop of a hat
I can cure
What the finest physicians have . . .
BROWNING (*turning at the desk*)
Say that you will and believe that you will
And I not only think it
I'm *sure*!
Want to be well
That is the goal
Deep in your heart
And your soul
Try to be well
Take it on trust
Mean to be well
(*He moves* C)
And you must
"Yes" is the word that you need
Know that you're going to succeed
ELIZABETH.
Talk's not the same as a deed
BROWNING.
Want to be well and you can
Be a man!

(*He sits on the* R *end of the sofa*)

ELIZABETH (*spoken*) My dear Mr Browning . . .
BROWNING.
If you'll only
Pretend to be well
Banish the pain
Cherish the thought
In your brain
Tell the rest of the
(*He rises to* C)
World that you're well
Summon a crowd

Swear it and shout
It aloud
ELIZABETH.
Oh, what a vision to hold!
BROWNING.
Fate always favours the bold
Tell your*self*—and then do as you're told!
Want to be well
And it's done!
You've won!

ELIZABETH (*spoken*) You frighten me.
BROWNING (*moving above the sofa*) Give me your hands. (*He takes both her hands in his*) Can't you feel new life surging into your heart and brain?
ELIZABETH (*shaken*) Please let go.

(BROWNING *opens his hands; but* ELIZABETH *still leaves hers lying on his palms for a moment. Then she withdraws them and, clasping her cheeks, looks at him with distracted eyes*)

BROWNING (*gently*) It's not me you're afraid of, it's life.
ELIZABETH. Well, when life becomes a series of electric shocks . . .
BROWNING. Was it as bad as all that?
ELIZABETH (*smiling*) Do you affect other people the same way?
BROWNING. They've often told me so. (*He sits on the* R *end of the sofa*) Will you do as I say? Think as I think?
ELIZABETH. I doubt if my father would approve of that. He— he has strong views himself.
BROWNING. Stronger than mine?
ELIZABETH (*looking at him; slowly*) I'm not sure which is the stronger—you or father.
BROWNING (*rising to* C*; grimly, with confidence*) We shall see. Do you trust me?

(*There is a second's pause*)

ELIZABETH. I trust you, yes . . .

REPRISE "I SAID LOVE"   No.
                              13

(BROWNING *moves to the table for his book and gloves. He listens to Elizabeth, turned away from her*)
(*singing*)   You said love—can this be love?
                   For it's clear from the start
                   Something very strange has happened
                   Happened here in my heart.
BROWNING.
                   Far away down the ages
                   This was planned and decreed

Elizabeth.
         Like a book with the pages
         Only meant for us to read
Browning.
         I said love and I mean love
         I repeat from the start—

(Browning *turns to her*)

Browning *and* Elizabeth (*singing together*)
         Something wonderful has happened
         Happened here in my heart

Browning *bows and goes out.* Elizabeth *looks after him—with love, as the* Lights *fade.*

Scene 6

The Hall of Number Fifty, Wimpole Street

When the Lights *come up the* Family *are discovered, bursting with curiosity, as follows:* Alfred *down* r, Arabel *at the harmonium,* Henrietta *up* l *of Alfred,* Charles *up* lc, George l *of Charles,* Barrett *sitting down* l *reading a newspaper. The music continues to play while* Browning *enters down the stairs, bows to the children, and comes face to face with Barrett.* Barrett *lowers his newspaper and rises.* Browning *bows low, and moves to the front door.* George *opens the door.* Browning *exits.* George *closes the door and moves to* l *of Henrietta.* Barrett *stares after Browning.* Arabel *plays with renewed fervour.*

REPRISE "LOVE AND DUTY"   No.
                                 14

Brothers *and* Sisters (*singing together; joyfully*)
         Love and duty fill this house
         Warm the wainscote
         Heat the hearth
         Bar the door to hate and guile
         Envy with her mocking laugh.

(Barrett *eyes them coldly, then exits upstairs.* Wilson *enters up* c. Alfred *meets her down* rc *and whirls her round*)

Wilson.   Honour be my faithful friend
                 Virtue is its own reward
                 As my daily task I tend
Charles (*moving* l *of Wilson and looking at his watch*)
                 Time to walk the dog
Wilson.   Dear Lord!

(Wilson *exits up* l. *The* Lights *dim to* Black-out. *The* Music *continues. During the following sequence, which is a stylized Musical Montage of the next few months, the Hall of Fifty Wimpole*

*Street is seen simultaneously with a series of impressionistic glimpses
of the world outside:-*
A flower-shop counter appears down L, *with an* ASSISTANT *standing
above it, and* BROWNING R *of her.* COOK *stands* C. BROWNING *is
being served by the* ASSISTANT)

ASSISTANT. Thank you, sir. I'll send them at once.

(BROWNING *starts to leave* R. COOK *moves to* R *of the* ASSISTANT)

And now, sir, the name of *your* lady?
COOK. Miss Moulton-Barrett.

(BROWNING *stops* C)

ASSISTANT (*to Cook*) Address?
COOK
BROWNING } (*together*) { Fifty Wimpole Street.

(COOK *and* BROWNING *stare at each other*)

COOK (*stiffly*) Miss Henrietta?
BROWNING. Miss Elizabeth.
COOK (*beaming*) Oh! That's all right, then. (*He clicks his heels
together*) Cook, Captain, Household Cavalry.
BROWNING (*tongue in cheek*) Browning, poet, household word.
(*With a cheerful wave at Cook he sails out of the shop*)

(*The* MUSIC *continues. The* ASSISTANT *and* COOK *exit down* L.
The shop counter is taken off. BROWNING *enters the Hall of the house,
where the* FAMILY *are grouped round the harmonium.* BROWNING
places his hat and gloves on the table up C *and exits quickly upstairs*)

THE FAMILY (*singing gaily*)
          Sex is not permissible
          If you're kissable
          Kindly go away.

(BARRETT *enters up* C *and stops by the table. The* FAMILY *freeze
when they see him. Thoughtfully, he picks up Browning's gloves and
stares up the stairs. The* LIGHTS *fade. The* MUSIC *continues.*
In the BLACK-OUT, BARRETT *sits down* L *and* WILSON *comes* C.
The LIGHTS *come up*)

WILSON (*to Barrett and the Family*) She's asked for a steak!

(*The* LIGHTS *fade to* BLACK-OUT. *The* MUSIC *continues. When
they come up again there is a knock at the front door.* WILSON *answers
it and returns with two bouquets, which are passed from one to the
other of the* FAMILY. BARRETT *comes down* C. CHARLES *takes the
larger bouquet to Barrett. Wilson moves to* R *of Barrett.* BARRETT
gives Wilson the bouquet, coldly. WILSON *exits upstairs,* BARRETT
exits up C)

"YOU ONLY TO LOVE ME"

(Henrietta *comes down* c, *taking the second bouquet from behind her back and looking lovingly at the card attached to it*)

Henrietta (*singing*)
> You only to love me
> You only to care
> Your smile in the morning
> Your step on the stair.
> My knowing you long for me
> The way I long for you
> Happens to a few
> We are two
> Of the rare ones
>
> You only to need me,
> My wish to be there
> No matter the why or when or where
> Don't bother to search for reasons
> Never mind the how
> But, oh, love, if you love me—
> Love me now!

(*The* Lights *fade. The* Music *continues.* Henrietta *rejoins the group.* Arabel *moves up* l. *A Travel Agency appears down* r. *When the* Lights *come up,* Browning *enters down* l *and crosses to the Agency. He takes an elaborate illustrated folder on the back of which, in bold lettering, is one word—*Italy. *He moves upstage and gives his hat, stick and coat to Alfred, then turns to Arabel up* l *and kisses her hand.* Browning *exits upstairs as* Arabel *faints into the arms of* George. *The* Lights *fade. The* Music *continues.*

As the Lights *come up, there is a knock on the front door.* Wilson *enters and opens it to a messenger who delivers a thin, narrow parcel, which is passed round in mystification.* Charles *takes it down* rc *miming a flute;* Alfred *moves* r *of Charles and takes it, miming a back-scratcher.* Wilson *takes the parcel from Alfred to* George *down* l. George *takes it and mimes a sunshade.* Wilson *takes the parcel and exits upstairs.* Dr Chambers *enters downstairs and opens the french windows* r)

REPRISE "THE WORLD OUTSIDE"

Chambers (*singing*)
> Nothing as blue as sky is
> Nothing as gentle as July is
> Whispering sounds of summer to
> The world outside
>
> Nothing as fair as dawn is
> Nothing as fresh and newly born is
> Scattering golden glory
> Far and wide

You have your own quiet room
Your very special private place
But when you know the sun again
And feel its glow upon your face
Gone all your fears
Gone every haunting shadow
Gone for ever
Nothing as soft as spring is
Nothing as green as each green thing is
Ready to view and waiting for you with pride
In that bright
New, wonderful world outside.

As the music builds to a climax, BARRETT *appears on the stairs with* ELIZABETH *in his arms. She wears a gay spring dress and looks a totally different being. The* FAMILY *and* WILSON *watch motionless as* BARRETT *carries Elizabeth tenderly across to* R *and through the french windows, followed by* DR CHAMBERS. *The* FAMILY *and* WILSON *stand together* C *as the scene changes to—*

SCENE 7
The sun-drenched garden of Number Fifty, Wimpole Street

All is light and air and fresh white blossom. The contrast with the Victorian interior is blinding. The garden wall stretches across the width of the stage. Angled behind it are the tall storied houses adjoining. There is an entrance from a mews L, *and some garden steps down* L *leading up to the back of the stables at the foot of the garden.*

As the scene opens, TRAVERS, *a gardener, brings a wheel-chair from up* L *to* RC. BARRETT *enters* R *through the french windows carrying* ELIZABETH *and followed by* DR CHAMBERS. BARRETT *moves* R *of the wheel-chair and puts* ELIZABETH *into it.* DR CHAMBERS *stands* L *of the chair.*

CHAMBERS. My dear Miss Barrett, I congratulate you!
THE FAMILY *and* WILSON (*applauding*) Hear, hear, bravo Miss Ba! Good for you, well done, old girl, etc.
BARRETT. Elizabeth, I thank God with all my heart that my ceaseless prayers have at last been answered.
ELIZABETH. Papa—er, Dr Chambers . . .
CHAMBERS. Mr Barrett, could I have a word with you, sir?
ELIZABETH (*eagerly*) Papa, Dr Chambers wants to ask you . . .
BARRETT (*smiling*) Perhaps we should let the good doctor tell me himself what he wants. I will leave you with your brothers and sisters. (*To the Family*) Do not tire her.
FAMILY. No, sir. Indeed, no, sir. Rather not, etc.
BARRETT (*to Chambers*) Perhaps you will be good enough to come to my study?

CHAMBERS. By all means.

(BARRETT *exits through the french windows* R)

(*To Elizabeth*) I'm delighted with your improvement, delighted. Enjoy the sun.

ELIZABETH. You will persuade him, won't you?

CHAMBERS. Leave it to me. I shall be firm, I promise you! (*He crosses* R *above the chair, then pauses*) Very—er—firm!

(CHAMBERS *exits* R. TRAVERS *moves to* L *of Elizabeth*)

TRAVERS (*touching his cap*) Lovely morning, miss.

ELIZABETH. Travers! How good to see you again! And how well you look! How well everything looks today.

TRAVERS. What you might call a regular poem of a morning, miss.

ELIZABETH (*radiant*) Better—far, far better, Travers—than all the poems ever written!

"THE REAL THING"   No. 15

(*Sung by* ELIZABETH, *and danced and sung by her* BROTHERS, SISTERS, FRIENDS *and* NEIGHBOURS. *The* FRIENDS *and* NEIGHBOURS *appear from the houses overlooking the garden and from the mews, and join in the song and dance*)

(*singing*)
I've read many panegyrics of delight
On the coming of the early tender shoot
But the finest is the merest substitute, my friend
For the real thing

ENSEMBLE.
What's the real thing?

ELIZABETH.
Why, the real thing
That's Spring
I've seen all that Mr Browning cared to write
I have poem after poem on the shelf
I've even written one or two myself, my friend
But not the real thing

ENSEMBLE.
What's the real thing?

ELIZABETH.
Why, the real thing
That's Spring

A VOICE (*spoken*)
Spring? What's Spring?

ELIZABETH.
Spring's a singing in the air
Spring's a stirring in the soil

Spring's a budding of a rose without a thorn
ENSEMBLE.
Spring's a message, it's a hope
Spring's the feeling you can cope
ELIZABETH.
Because a brand new, grand new world's been born.

(CHARLES *moves the wheel-chair to* C)

ENSEMBLE.
Halleluia! Halleluia!
Halleluia! Halleluia! Halleluia!
ELIZABETH.
I thought living could be done at second-hand
Through a novel or a painting or a play
But they none of them compare in any way, my friend
With the real thing.
And what's the real thing?
ENSEMBLE.
Why, the real thing—that's Spring!
A VOICE (*spoken*)
"Drink deep—or taste not the Pierian Spring"
FEMALES.
Spring! Is not a hole for water
ELIZABETH.
Spring! Is not a glass of porter
MALES.
Spring! Is when you have a daughter
FEMALES.
I may have a son.
MALES.
How many?
FEMALES.
Just one.
MALES.
You're not concentrating.
ENSEMBLE.
Spring! Is when you kiss a stranger
Spring! Is when it's green for danger
OCTAVIUS (*spoken*)
Spring is when you g-get out of bed
and s-stand on your head
ELIZABETH (*spoken*) Precisely, Occy. (*Singing*)
Spring's a buzzing in the brain
Spring's a tingling in the toes
Spring's a time to take a husband or a wife
ENSEMBLE.
Spring's a kicking up of legs
It's a drinking to the dregs

ELIZABETH.
Of the latest, greatest thing called life

(HENRY *takes the wheel-chair down* R *for the ballet*)

ENSEMBLE.
Halleluia! Halleluia!
Halleluia! Halleluia! Halleluia!

SPRING BALLET   No. 15a

(*A major dance sequence,* THE SPRING BALLET, *develops. As it finishes,* HENRY *brings the wheel-chair* C *and the entire* COMPANY *form a group round it*)

CODA "THE REAL THING"   No. 15b

ELIZABETH (*singing*)
Without rhyme or reason Spring can make you laugh
Or alternatively move you close to tears
Especially if it's been your first for years, my friend
But today—no
When a halo
Rings a rainbow high above
That's the right time
For the real thing
ENSEMBLE.
What's the real thing?
ALL.
That's love!

LINK AFTER "THE REAL THING"   No. 15c

(*The* FRIENDS, NEIGHBOURS *and* FAMILY *form a ring round Elizabeth and continue their dance.* CHARLES *gets a small chair from off* L *and sits* R *of Elizabeth.* BARRETT *enters* R *and moves to* R *of the group. The dance stops instantly. The* FRIENDS *and* NEIGHBOURS *exit, leaving the* FAMILY)

BARRETT (*furiously*) I specifically told you not to tire your sister. Yet I find you romping round her like a lot of disorderly children. I am most displeased.

(CHARLES, *with his back to Barrett, mimics him, which makes* HENRIETTA *give a nervous giggle*)

I am not aware that I have said anything amusing, Henrietta.
HENRIETTA. I'm sorry, Papa.
BARRETT. Very well. (*To the Family*) You may go.

(*The* FAMILY *exit* R, *with alacrity*)

ELIZABETH. Papa, did—did Dr Chambers speak to you about—next winter?

BARRETT. Dr Chambers talked, if I may say so, a great deal of nonsense.

ELIZABETH (*nervously*) But—didn't he tell you that I should avoid spending next winter in England and that he thinks I'll be fit to travel to Italy in October—he often goes there himself and he feels that the climate would be benefic . . .

BARRETT. So! The precious plot is out at last! And your brothers and sisters—do they know of this delightful plan?

ELIZABETH. I believe I mentioned it to them.

BARRETT. You believe you mentioned it to them. And that charlatan Browning—no doubt you also mentioned it to him? Or was that unnecessary—was it his idea?

ELIZABETH. What does it matter whose idea it was?

BARRETT. Matter? Not in the least! It's nothing at all that I alone should be shut out of your confidence—treated like a cipher . . .

ELIZABETH. Believe me, my one reason for not worrying you with this Italian idea before was . . .

BARRETT. The fear that I should nip it in the bud. Exactly.

ELIZABETH. No, Papa, I . . .

BARRETT. Please. Spare me further excuses. I am cut to the heart that you—the only one of my children whom I trusted implicitly—should be capable of such underhand conduct.

ELIZABETH. There was nothing underhand . . .

BARRETT. Did it never occur to you that all through those long dark months you proposed to enjoy yourself in Italy—a grossly overrated country, by the way, nothing but dust, flies, stenches and beggars—did it never cross your mind that your father would be left here utterly alone?

ELIZABETH. But how can you say that? The rest of the family . . .

BARRETT. Your brothers and sisters might as well be shadows for all the companionship they afford me. Edward—the only child other than yourself I ever cared for—Edward is dead. And you—oh, don't think that I haven't noticed that you, now that you are stronger and no longer wholly dependent on me, are slowly drawing away from your father.

ELIZABETH. It's not true!

BARRETT. Little by little, I am being pushed into the background—I, who used to be your whole world, I, your father, who loves you . . .

ELIZABETH. But nothing has changed—nothing has altered. My love for you . . .

BARRETT. Is apparently non-existent. You ask for my consent

to this—Italian jaunt. I neither give it nor withhold it. You are
at liberty to do as you wish. But if you go, I hope you will some-
times spare a thought for your father. Think of him perhaps at
night, going upstairs into that room which once held all he
cared for on this earth.

(BROWNING *appears suddenly from the house* R)

BROWNING (*his eyes lighting up at the sight of Elizabeth*) Bravo!
Bravo! Bravissimo! Welcome back to the world at large! A
thousand welcomes! (*To Barrett*) Sir, I take my oath, you're the
happiest father in the land.

BARRETT. In that case, sir, you perjure yourself.

(BARRETT *goes into the house* R. BROWNING *stares after him,
frowning*)

ELIZABETH. He doesn't mean to be rude, it's just that he's
over-anxious . . .

BROWNING (*sitting* R *of Elizabeth*) Anxious? And so am I.
(*Turning to her eagerly*) Tell me quickly—Italy—Chambers agrees
to your wintering there?

ELIZABETH. Yes, but . . .

BROWNING. Splendid. When does he think you'll be fit to
travel?

ELIZABETH. October—unless there's a relapse, but . . .

BROWNING. Relapse? There's no such word! October! Now
there's a coincidence. I've made up my mind to remodel *Sordello*.
That can't be done in England. Impossible to get the true
Italian atmosphere. October will suit me perfectly. Where will
you be staying?

ELIZABETH (*quietly*) Here—at Fifty Wimpole Street.

BROWNING. But—you just told me that Chambers . . .

ELIZABETH. Doctors propose—Father—disposes.

BROWNING. He's forbidden it?

ELIZABETH. Let's say—he's made it impossible for me to go.

BROWNING. But, in Heaven's name, why?

ELIZABETH (*quickly, nervously*) You see, he's very devoted to me
and . . .

BROWNING. Devoted!

ELIZABETH. Very—and if I were away for six months . . .

BROWNING (*visibly and audibly restraining himself*) Miss Barrett,
may I speak plainly?

ELIZABETH. Please don't.

BROWNING. Very well. (*Suddenly his control gives way and he
bursts out in a torrent of words. Rising*) No, by God, I will! You say
he's devoted. I don't understand a devotion that demands duty,
respect, obedience and love and gives nothing in return—a
devotion that spends itself in petty tyrannies and bullying and

doesn't even stop at risking your life to gratify its colossal selfishness! If that's devotion, then give me good, sound, honest hatred!

ELIZABETH. Please . . .

BROWNING (*kneeling* R *of Elizabeth*) It's not just your happiness that's at stake. It's your life. I forbid you to play with your life!

ELIZABETH. Don't go on, don't go on . . .

BROWNING. And *I* have the right to forbid you. (*With total certainty*) I loved you before I met you—I love you now and I shall love you to the end. You know that?

ELIZABETH (*brokenly*) Yes—yes—I've always known. And now —please go. We must never see each other again.

BROWNING (*drawing her into his arms*) Elizabeth, I love you. I want you for my wife.

ELIZABETH (*resisting feebly*) No—Robert, no . . .

(BROWNING *kisses her on the lips. Suddenly her arms go round his neck*)

Oh, Robert, Robert—I . . .

BROWNING. Go on, say it.

ELIZABETH. I can't. I can't find the words—new words, special, splendid, wonderful words.

BROWNING. The simplest will do.

"IN A SIMPLE WAY"   No. 16

ELIZABETH (*singing*)
    I love you
    I love you
    Oh, my darling, I do
    In a simple way
    You'll observe with surprise
    There are stars in my eyes
    Pardon my cliché
    To convey what you feel
    When the feeling is real
    And your heart is aglow
    There's no phrase that's so right
    Or more truly delightful
    Than I love you so
    In a simple way

    You can write it in prose
    You can sing it in verse
BROWNING (*rising*)
    It's so beautifully brief
ELIZABETH.
    So deliciously terse

Browning.
    And as easy to say
    As for better for worse
    As you will one day
Elizabeth (*spoken*) I must go in now.
Browning (*spoken*) Elizabeth, listen to me.

(*He sings in mock Italian style*)

    As I said-a before
    Let me show you amor
    The Italian way
    Toss-a coins in-a fountains
    You climb seven mountains
    Of Rome next day
    (*He pushes the wheel-chair down* R)
    Make-a love in a gondola
    After-a dark
Elizabeth (*entering into the spirit*)
    Watch-a pigeons a fluttering
    Round-a St Mark
Browning.
    Take what Venice can give
Elizabeth.
    And see Naples
Browning.
    And *live!* The Italian Way.

    Elizabella mia, why you not hear my call?
    Is evident to see-a you no love-a me at all
    From Napoli to Roma, see, the olive groves repine
    Come leave-a your old home-a and—mia—be-a mine!
(*Spoken*) Viva Napoli! Viva Firenze! Viva Pisa!
Elizabeth (*spoken*) Ssh! Father will hear you.
Browning (*spoken*) *Bene! Bene! Benone!* Elizabella mia—do
you know what Italia will do for you?
Elizabeth (*spoken*) No.
Browning (*singing*)
    Put-a rose in your cheek
    Not-a once in a while
    Every day of the week
    And-a permanent smile
    And what's more . . .
Elizabeth (*singing*) If I might be permitted to speak!
Browning (*spoken*) *Si, signorina.*
Elizabeth (*spoken*) *Grazie.*
Browning (*spoken*) *Prego!*

ELIZABETH (*singing*)
>What a madly impossible person you are!

BROWNING (*singing*)
>*Impossibile?* Never!
>You follow your star
>Crying "*a rivederci!*
>To hell with Papa!*"*

ELIZABETH (*spoken*) Robert!

BROWNING (*singing*) In the nicest way.

ELIZABETH (*spoken*) Oh, Robert, Robert, I adore you.

BROWNING (*spoken*) Is-a *bene.*

ELIZABETH *and* BROWNING (*singing together*)
>When you fly down the street
>And can't speak when you meet
>That's the simple way

BROWNING.
>You leap over a wall
>For no reason at all
>And exclaim:

ELIZABETH *and* BROWNING (*together*)
>Hooray!

ELIZABETH.
>It's a wonderful world
>And it's suddenly clear

BROWNING.
>That to rhyme moon and June
>Is a brilliant idea

ELIZABETH *and* BROWNING (*together*)
>In a flash you discover
>The words every lover
>Delights to hear

BROWNING.
>They're as clear as a bell

ELIZABETH.
>They're as fresh as the dew

BROWNING.
>They're as old as the hills

ELIZABETH.
>They're eternally new.

ELIZABETH *and* BROWNING (*together*)
>And they say what I feel in
>My heart about you.

ELIZABETH.
>In an easy

BROWNING.
>Normal

ELIZABETH.
>Natural

ELIZABETH *and* BROWNING (*together*)
Simple way.
BROWNING.
If you've something to say
It will probably pay
If you say it that way
ELIZABETH *and* BROWNING (*together*)
Olè!

ELIZABETH. You must go now.
BROWNING. Until tomorrow.
ELIZABETH. No, out of my life.
BROWNING. With those words singing in my ears? (*Staring at her*) This is life—*life* offering us the best there is. What are you? A coward?
ELIZABETH. Yes, I'm a coward. But it's not for myself I'm afraid. As your wife, I should always be an invalid, you know that . . .
BROWNING (*kneeling* L *of her*) No, I don't know that. There's nothing physically wrong. You have eyes—they can see. You have lips—they can speak. You have arms—they can hold. You have feet—they can walk.
ELIZABETH. One day, perhaps.
BROWNING. Whenever you really want them to. (*He rises and moves* C. *Suddenly*) Get up, Elizabeth.
ELIZABETH (*startled*) What?
BROWNING. Get up.
ELIZABETH. I can't.
BROWNING. *I* think you can.
ELIZABETH (*afraid*) No. Robert, please, don't make me . . .
BROWNING. No one can *make* you do anything. But *you* can make your*self*—if you want to.
ELIZABETH (*trying to rise*) It's no use, I can't.
BROWNING. You can, you *must*. I *need* you.

(ELIZABETH *stares at him. He moves to her to hold the chair. She tries to rise, and fails. She tries again—and again falls back. At last, with his help, she gets slowly, painfully, to her feet. She sways a little, clings to him*)
(*Supporting her*) Giddy?
ELIZABETH (*breathless with the effort*) A little.
BROWNING (*almost equally breathless with excitement*) Close your eyes and lean against me. Better?
ELIZABETH. Yes.
BROWNING. Now—we're going to walk together. Walk with me, Elizabeth.
ELIZABETH. It's my knees. They don't seem able to—to support me.
BROWNING. I'm here. I won't let you go. Now—walk with me.

(BROWNING *starts to walk backwards, holding her hands. She takes a couple of faltering steps, then stops*)

(*Quickly*) No—don't look down. (*He takes her arms and walks in front of her*) Keep your eyes on mine. That's right—look at me.

(ELIZABETH *starts to move forward again. They move slowly to* C)

ELIZABETH. Robert, I'm sure I can't manage . . .
BROWNING. You *are* walking.

(*Very gradually,* BROWNING *releases her hands and moves up* L. *She takes two more small steps to* LC—*and realizes. Tremulous, aglow, she faces him*)

ELIZABETH. But how—how . . .?
BROWNING (*quietly, triumphantly*) Don't you know?
ELIZABETH (*deeply in love*) Yes, oh yes . . .

"I KNOW NOW"

No.
17

(*singing*)
I know now
Why all the world is fine and fair
And why there's music in the air
To listen to

(BROWNING *moves to Elizabeth and puts his arm round her waist*)

BROWNING (*singing*)
If all the world is fine and fair
And if there's music in the air
ELIZABETH *and* BROWNING (*singing together*)
The song is you.
ELIZABETH.
I know now
Why there are ripples on a stream
And why it's wonderful to dream
As dreamers do
BROWNING.
If there are ripples on a stream
And when it's wonderful to dream
ELIZABETH *and* BROWNING (*together*)
The dream is you.
BROWNING.
You're shadow when it's warm
ELIZABETH.
You're shelter from a storm
ELIZABETH *and* BROWNING (*together*)
You're every lovely form
I ever knew
And so now

When they say heaven's high above
I wonder what they're thinking of
It can't be true
There is no heaven high above
Heaven is somebody to love
As I love you.
BROWNING.
    You're every smile that's smiled
ELIZABETH.
    The winter when it's wild
ELIZABETH and BROWNING (*together*)
A lark that's been beguiled
Beyond the blue

And so now
When they say heaven's far away
If there is truth in what they say
There must be two
The one that's far away above
The one that's having you to love
My whole life through
This I know now
And so, I know, do you.

(BROWNING *and* ELIZABETH *embrace passionately. She breaks and takes one or two steps.* BARRETT *enters from the house* R)

BARRETT (*moving* RC) Elizabeth!

BROWNING. It's all right. Don't interfere, I beg you.

BARRETT. Are you mad? She's risking her life!

BROWNING. She's beginning to live her life for the first time. Can't you see?

BARRETT. What are you saying? She has no life—except what I give her. Her only strength is my strength.

BROWNING. Not any more. Show him, Elizabeth. Show him you can stand on your own feet. Show him you're free of him.

BARRETT. What monstrous lie has this man been telling you?

ELIZABETH (*facing her father*) I'm well. Surely you can see that I'm well.

BARRETT. It's only by God's mercy you're not lying dead.

BROWNING. Barrett, if you have a grain of imagination, I implore you . . .

ELIZABETH. It's all right. I *can* walk. Look. (*She starts to walk slowly, determinedly, towards her father*)

BARRETT (*quietly tense*) I lost one child because he took an insane risk, wasn't that enough?

(ELIZABETH *stops, but steels herself and takes another step towards Barrett*)

(*Deliberately*) Elizabeth, *wasn't Edward's death enough?*

CURTAIN MUSIC   No.
                             17a

(At the mention of Edward's name ELIZABETH *stops dead. There is a pause. She sways, and faints.* BARRETT *catches her.* BROWNING *runs forward and kneels* L *of Elizabeth)*

BARRETT *(violently)* Leave her to me!

(BARRETT *picks Elizabeth up.* BROWNING *rises and backs* C)

(To Elizabeth) You're safe, my darling.

(BARRETT *turns to Browning, who stands rooted)*

You will not come here again on any pretext whatsoever. Do you understand me? Get out of this house. Get out of our lives!

BARRETT *carries* ELIZABETH *slowly into the house, leaving* BROWNING *alone in the garden, as—*

the CURTAIN *falls*

ENTR'ACTE   No.
                             17b

ACT II

Scene i

Elizabeth's Room

When the Curtain *rises,* Elizabeth *is discovered lying on her couch in the same dress as Act I Scene 3. She is finishing a tankard of porter.* Barrett *stands above the sofa, watching her. She finishes the drink.*

Barrett. Good. (*He takes the tankard and puts it on the cupboard in the alcove*) Did you have a pleasant day, my dear?
Elizabeth. The same as usual, Papa.
Barrett. Then you had a pleasant day.
Elizabeth. If you say so, Papa.
Barrett. You must try not to be bitter, Elizabeth.
Elizabeth. I'm not bitter, Papa. Just realistic.
Barrett. Shall I come and see you later and say good night?
Elizabeth. As you wish.
Barrett. After all these months of estrangement it is for *you* to say that *you* wish it.

(*There is a silence*)

Very well. (*He turns to go*)

(Elizabeth *picks up an opened letter from the table below the sofa.* Barrett *stops inquiringly*)

Elizabeth (*wearily*) From Miss Mitford, Father. Mr Browning continues to respect your wishes—and mine. As you know very well, I have neither seen nor heard from him for many months. Please read it yourself, if you doubt my word. (*She holds out the letter*)
Barrett. I have never doubted your word, Elizabeth. That is not our relationship.

(Barrett *exits* r)

"SOLILOQUY"

No.
18

Elizabeth (*singing*)
    Tied to a sofa in an airless room
    Like Andromeda chained to a rock
    While the seasons fly and the days drift by
    To the aimless tick of the clock
    And the Doctors call and puzzle and frown
    And strike a professional pose
    And one says this and the other says that
    As they dither and differ a.id diagnose

But for all their chatter
The truth of the matter
Is no one really knows
What's wrong
Nobody really knows
What's wrong with me?
In ten years you may be well, they say
What's wrong with me?
Ten years! That's almost a century!
What's wrong with me?
Why do my arms and legs and feet decline to do
What every fibre of my being begs them to
Even a dog can move at will
Even a child of three can stand
Must I be like this
Alone in all the land?
Is it so very much to ask?
Such an extravagant demand?
Why am I helpless
Without a helping hand?

I wasn't always like this. When I was
small I was lithe, and strong, and rather
wild. A tom-boy, in fact. I doubt
you'd have known me.

Like a boy I took to the trees
Like a boy I rode and I ran
And tumbled and fought
And the family thought
She'll grow up to be a man

Quick-silver swift was I
And as boisterous as they came
And you'd never have thought
I'd a thought in my head
Or a poem to my name

Black and blue from the fights I'd had
With the neighbours and friends next door
If anyone said
It was time for bed
I'd protest "Just one fight more!"
Not a care in the world had I
Nor an introspective fear
I was supple and strong
As the days were long
Until Edward died

And then something inside—
Well, nothing was quite the same since Edward,
No, nothing was quite the same.

And now I'm a woman of parts
With a talent to rhyme and scan
And now I can do what few can do
But not what everyone can
For a long time it didn't seem to matter
Not really,
Until you came, Robert.

When you came
Another air blew through the room
A blazing light lit up the gloom
And filled the sky
My heart was high
And hope was new
The wildest dream I dreamed came true
The day you came

(She puts her feet on the floor)
With your help
I found the strength to leave my cell
I felt so certain I was well
And, oh, my dear,
Just for a moment it was true
Just for a moment love I knew
(She rises)
For you were there

Want to be well!
I want it so
(She takes four paces to c)
This much I know
Don't ask me how
It will be never
Or I vow, it shall be
Now!

(On the last triumphant note, ELIZABETH *realizes that somehow, miraculously, she is on her feet. She staggers to the table* c, *then to the chair at the desk* R *and leans on it. There is a tap at the door.* HENRI-ETTA *enters without seeing Elizabeth immediately; she closes the door and turns up the gas bracket beside it)*

HENRIETTA. Ba, we've just had a family conference—minus Father, needless to say—and we've come to the conclu . . .

(*She looks towards the sofa, then turns and sees Elizabeth by the desk*)
Ba! (*She runs and embraces Elizabeth*) Darling, darling, darling Ba!

(ELIZABETH *and* HENRIETTA *cling in a wild embrace. At length, gasping,* HENRIETTA *holds her sister at arm's length*)

Don't move, don't go away. (*She flies to the door, opens it and calls off* R) George! Charles! Alfred! Everyone! Quick! Quick! (*She runs above the sofa*) But how—*how*?
ELIZABETH (*still dazed*) I don't know.

(GEORGE *hurries in, followed by* HENRY *and* ALFRED. GEORGE *moves above the sofa,* HENRY *to* R *of George,* ALFRED *to the* R *end of the sofa*)

GEORGE. What's wrong?
HENRY. You all right, old girl?
ALFRED. Something up?
HENRIETTA. Yes, Ba.
GEORGE. Good God! (*He sits upstage on the sofa*)

(ALFRED *crosses up* R. *They all gape.* OCTAVIUS, CHARLES *and* SEPTIMUS *pile through the door*)

OCTAVIUS (*moving to the down* R *corner of the sofa*) W-what's all the d-din ab-b-b . . . (*He turns, sees Elizabeth, and sits*)

(*They all stare*)

CHARLES (*moving to the* R *end of the sofa*) Well, I'm damned!
SEPTIMUS (*moving below the table* C) Done it at last. (*He draws Elizabeth downstage of the table*)
OCTAVIUS. It's a m-m-m-m-m-m-m-

(CHARLES *hits Octavius on the shoulder to stop him stammering, then sits above him*)

-miracle!!

(WILSON *enters. If she had a tray she would drop it*)

WILSON. Merciful Heaven!

(WILSON *moves* C. SEPTIMUS *moves* LC, HENRY *above the table,* GEORGE *rises and goes up* L)

ELIZABETH (*firmly*) Wilson, help me to change.

(*During the following speeches* WILSON *takes* ELIZABETH *into the alcove up* L *and* HENRIETTA *draws the curtain half across it*)

WILSON. Are you feeling all right, miss?
ELIZABETH. I've never felt better in my life!
WILSON (*staring at Elizabeth*) Are you dreaming or is it me?

(HENRIETTA *gives a whoop of joy and follows them into the alcove. The* BROTHERS *turn to one another, suddenly feeling the full impact of Elizabeth's recovery*)

OCTAVIUS (*anxiously*) Do you think she will be all r-right this time? I mean, she won't have a r-relapse?

(GEORGE *sits on the sofa,* ALFRED *stands below the door* C, HENRY *at the desk* R, CHARLES *down* L. SEPTIMUS *sits* L *of the table* C, OCTAVIUS *sits on the alcove chair*)

GEORGE. No, but I may.

ALFRED. I can feel one coming on myself.

HENRY. Yes.

CHARLES. Hear, hear!

"PASS THE EAU DE COLOGNE"   No. 19

ALFRED (*singing*)
  Pass the Eau de Cologne, for God's sake!

(CHARLES *takes the bottle of Eau de Cologne from the dresser in the window and throws it to Alfred*)

  The Sal Volatile, *please!*
ALL.
  Elizabeth's on her feet, boys
  Elizabeth's off her knees
HENRY.
  To echo the ranks of Tuscany
  We can scarce forbear to cheer
ALFRED.
  But the Eau de Cologne, if you *don't* mind.
CHARLES.
  And a couple of quarts of beer
ALL.
  I need the Eau de Cologne or you'll have me prone
CHARLES.
  And a barrel or two of beer!
SEPTIMUS.
  Pass the Sal Volatile, someone!
OCTAVIUS.
  The Eau de Cologne, I b-beg!
ALL.
  Elizabeth's on the move, boys
  Elizabeth's shown a leg
GEORGE.
  We shall have to tell Papa, boys
HENRY.
  He'll never survive the shock
GEORGE.
  So a couple of whiffs of ammonia

CHARLES.
And a couple of pints of hock
ALL.
I said, a dose in the nose of ammonia
CHARLES.
And a case or two of hock!
ALL.
In our stride we take whatever the papers say
But this news has caused an attack of the vapours!
ALFRED.
Hey!
The Sal Volatile, *grazie*!
SEPTIMUS.
The Eau de Cologne, *merci*!
ALL.
Our Betty is out of bed, boys
Our Lizzie is on the spree
HENRY.
When you've knocked me down with a feather
You can pick me up again.
ALL.
And it's opium pipes for everyone
CHARLES.
And a magnum of champagne!
ALL.
I said, it's opium pipes for the weaker types
But kiss me with cocaine!
GEORGE.
This Eau de Cologne's so soothing!
So flattering to the face!
Sister has had a siesta
ALFRED.
And rejoined the human race
ALL.
Oh, we knew that she had it in her
It was perfectly plain to see
Still, it's after you with the oxygen—
And is anyone here for tea?
GEORGE.
I said, you can bloody well queue for the oxygen—
'Cos the one who's fainting's me!
OCTAVIUS.
Could not be more stunned at the news we've heard today
If you'd told me Wilson was in the f-family way
ALFRED, HENRY *and* SEPTIMUS (*singing together*)
Some Eau de Cologne for you, Ba?
Le Sal Volatile?

(ELIZABETH *puts her head round the alcove curtain*)

ELIZABETH (*spoken*) No! I'm finished with pharmacopeia.
(*She disappears*)
ALL (*singing*)
    Well, doesn't it go to show?
    You never know what's in store, boys
    The moral is blazing bright
SEPTIMUS.
    If we're under the sod tomorrow
    We're on top of the world tonight!
ALL.
    I said, if it's back to the earth tomorrow
    It's a wonderful day tonight!

    All hail to our darling sister!
    All hail to our lovely Ba!
    She'd booked her date for the Pearly gates
    Where the other angels are
    When suddenly up she popped, boys
    The reason we can't compute
CHARLES.
    But blaze away with the Montrachet
    And a twenty-one gun salute!
ALL.
    I said, you can slake my thirst with a brandy burst
    And a regular royal salute!
    Shoot!

The LIGHTS *fade*

SCENE CHANGE MUSIC   **No.**
(Reprise from K)   **19**

SCENE 2

The Hall of Number Fifty Wimpole Street

As the LIGHTS *come up,* ARABEL *enters through the front door with a
pile of boxes and moves* LC. BELLA *follows, closes the door, and
moves* R *of Arabel.* BELLA *carries one small box.*

ARABEL (*exhausted*) Oh dear, oh dear, oh dear.
BELLA. Deawest Awabel —don't despair. You'll be mawwying
yourself—one day. (*She puts her one small box on Arabel's pile, puts
her handbag on the harmonium, takes out her mirror and looks at herself
as she hums the* "*Wedding March*")

(ARABEL *puts the boxes on the seat down* L)

Oh, I'm so pwetty! Never mind, Awabel, I'm sure you and

Henwietta will look wavishing as bwidesmaids. Don't you adore dwessing up?
ARABEL. I never "dress up", Bella.
BELLA. Never? But surely you're going to the fancy dwess ball at Cwemorne tomowwow night?
ARABEL. Fancy dress? Papa would die.
BELLA. But evewyone who is anyone will be there. I shall be there. I'm going as Titania, queen of the faiwies. Why don't you go as Cleopatwa? Perhaps some Anthony will come along and whisk you away.
ARABEL. Really, Bella.
BELLA. What's wong? Don't you dweam about being whisked away by men evewy night?
ARABEL. Certainly not. Not every night.
BELLA. You needn't be weserved with me. Until I met Hawwy, I adored all men indiscwiminately.
ARABEL (moving to Bella) Bella, I regret to say this, but you're one of the few girls I know who would have benefited entirely from Papa's system of upbringing.
BELLA. What a thwilling thought! He was fwightfully stwict, wasn't he? Did he whip you when you were disobedient?

(BARRETT enters up C)

I'd adore to be whipped by Uncle Edward. (She sees Barrett in her hand-mirror. With a start) There you are, Uncle. (She puts her mirror with the handbag on the harmonium)

(ARABEL takes one of the boxes from L and scurries upstairs like a frightened doe. BARRETT moves down C)

Oh! I love that stern and stwict exterior.

(BELLA moves R of Barrett and slips her arm through his)

Uncle dear, if I'd been your little girl instead of Papa's, would you have taken the stwap to me? You wouldn't, would you? Or would you?
BARRETT. Would—wouldn't—wouldn't—would? Are you trying to pose me with some silly riddle? (Noticing the parcels) What's all this paraphernalia?
BELLA. The girls' things for my wedding. But why that gloomy fwown, Uncle? (She passes her hands lightly over his forehead) There—there—all gone! Awabel says it would have done me all the good in the world to have been bwought up by you. She thinks I'm spoilt and fwivolous. What do you think? (She snuggles closer to him)
BARRETT. I think that if my children were as open and affectionate as you are, I should be a much happier man.
BELLA (turning her back to him) You mustn't say things like that, or they'll hate me.

BARRETT (*putting one arm round her waist and drawing her close*)
And you're a distractingly lovely little creature . . .
BELLA. Anything wong in that?
BARRETT (*taking his arm away*) I didn't say so.
BELLA. Then why do you look at me so fiercely?
BARRETT. What's that scent you have on you?
BELLA. Don't you like it?
BARRETT (*moving to the stool down* L) It's very delicate and
subtle. Still, I should prefer you not to use it.
BELLA. Why?
BARRETT (*picking up "Blackwood's Magazine" from the stool and
sitting on the* R *end of it*) Never mind!
BELLA (*triumphantly*) But I never use scent! I think it's howwid
and common. It's *me* you can smell!
BARRETT. Nonsense.
BELLA. It is! It's me! It's me!

"WHAT'S NATURAL"   No. 20

(*singing*)
What's natuwal may be stwong
What's sensuous can be shattewing
(*She moves* R *of Barrett*)
A foweign girl who woos a boy
May use some subtle twick or ploy
But never your English wose
Who just by wafting on the bweeze,
Makes gwown men go
Gwoggy at the knees
(*She crosses above the stool to* L *of it*)

She's delicate, she's discweet
Not wilfully aphwodisiac
(*Sitting* L *of Barrett*)
But when her fwagwance fills the skies
Gweat chaps collapse and dwop like flies
A bachelor may pwetend
You just can't push him off his perch
One whiff—
(*She rises*)
          —and he's waiting at the church
(*She crosses above the stool to* L *of it*)

The man who happens to be perfume pwone
Goes cwazy when your scent's your own
So if you're an English wose
You can't help conquewing the town
(*She sits on Barrett's knee*)

Your male inhales
Joy pwevails
Open the jails
Jewicho is down!

(BARRETT *throws Bella round on to his* L *knee and kisses her passionately. Then he abruptly pushes her off*)

BARRETT. Run along now, child.

(BARRETT *and* BELLA *rise.* BELLA *moves* R *for her handbag, then up* R *to the front door.* BARRETT *stays below the stool*)

I have to speak privately to my family . . .
BELLA (*turning at the front door*) Au wevoir—Uncle.

(BELLA *exits.* BARRETT *crosses down* R)

BARRETT. Good-bye.
ARABEL (*off; excitedly*) Papa! Papa! Where are you?

(ARABEL *appears at the top of the stairs and runs down to Barrett*)

Papa! Papa! She's up, she's up! She's coming down! She's up, Papa! (*She runs across down* L)
BARRETT. Up—down—up? Has the world gone mad this afternoon?

(*The* FAMILY *rush downstairs in the following order:* OCTAVIUS *to* L *of the front door,* SEPTIMUS *to up* R *of the foot of the stairs,* HENRY *to above Barrett,* CHARLES *to above Henry,* HENRIETTA *to* R *of Arabel,* GEORGE *to down* L *of the foot of the stairs.* ALFRED *precedes* ELIZABETH, *holding one of her hands. He stops* R *of the foot of the stairs and* ELIZABETH *comes down the last steps alone. She staggers, and* GEORGE *and* ALFRED *go to help her. Elizabeth waves them away and moves slowly down until she is up* L *of Barrett.* WILSON *follows the others and stays on the stairs*)

ELIZABETH (*at length*) I walked, Papa. I walked downstairs—alone.

(*There is a silence*)

Think, Father. Think what it means. I'm well.
BARRETT. These sudden rallies are not always the most favourable sign, as we have cause to remember. We mustn't set our hopes too high. It may be no more than a temporary phase.
ELIZABETH. Oh, this is not temporary, Father. I'm really well at last—I know—I can feel it. Just think—I'll be able to get out of that stifling room—go where I like—do what I like—breathe the fresh air . . .

(BARRETT *crosses the room in silence, to the fire-place.* ALL *watch him.* HENRY *moves down* R. BARRETT *turns*)

Barrett (*with precision*) By a happy chance you are about to have all the fresh air you can possibly want. I have just bought a house at Bookham, in Surrey, some twenty miles from London and six miles from Leatherhead, the nearest railway station.

(Charles *moves to support Elizabeth*)

On the twenty-second of this month, the entire family leaves Wimpole Street and moves to Bookham.

(*There is a gasp from the* Family)

Charles. Why?

Barrett (*ignoring this; to Elizabeth*) You will benefit not only from the country air but the complete seclusion of your new surroundings—complete, that is, apart from an adjacent nursing home, should we suffer a second setback. But I'm confident that can be avoided, provided you live quietly and sensibly in the country.

Elizabeth (*bitterly*) As distinct from my riotous life in town!

Barrett. There is a restlessness about London that is both physically and morally harmful.

Elizabeth (*moving* LC; *passionately*) But, Papa, I don't *want* to leave London!

Henrietta (*moving to Elizabeth*) No, none of us does.

Elizabeth. My friends are here . . .

George. Yes, sir, we all have friends here . . .

Henry. And London's our home!

Octavius (*moving down* R) We l-like it here.

Alfred (*moving up* L) Who wants the blasted country?

Septimus (*moving above Octavius*) Why should we move?

Charles. A bit sudden, isn't it, sir?

George. You might have warned us.

Barrett (*moving* C) I decline absolutely to discuss the matter.

Henrietta. Our whole lives uprooted, and you won't even discuss it!

Barrett (*turning to Henrietta on his* L) I'm not in the habit of accounting for my actions to anyone—least of all to my children.

Henrietta. We might as well be in jail!

Barrett. Be silent!

Henrietta. With our tongues cut out!

Barrett. Go to your room!

Henrietta. Not until you say *why!*

Barrett (*raising his hand to her*) Go to you room, girl, or by God, I'll . . .

Elizabeth (*stepping between them*) Papa!

(Barrett *lowers his hand*)

(*Quietly*) Come with me, Henrietta.

(ELIZABETH *puts her arm round* HENRIETTA, *and they exit upstairs.* WILSON *follows, then* ARABEL *scurries after them*)

ALFRED. Wasn't that rather unfair, sir?
GEORGE. We're not exactly children, you know, sir.
CHARLES. Or idiots.
BARRETT. I beg your pardon?
CHARLES. I said we're not fools, sir.
BARRETT. Is this some sort of rebellion?
SEPTIMUS. No, sir, but you might at least . . .
BARRETT (*with immense force*) Understand this! I and I alone will decide what's best for my family, and that decision, once made, will be accepted by every one of you, without debate, without argument, without question—whether you think it right or wrong.

"I'M THE MASTER HERE"   No.
                            21

(*singing*)
Wrong is right—if I say so
Black is white—if I say so
Day is night—if I say so
Is that clear?
(*To Septimus*)
You demurred, sir?
SEPTIMUS.
Not a word, sir.
(*He sits on the organ stool*)
BARRETT.
I'm the master here.
Well is ill—if I state it
Cure is kill—if I state it
As my will may dictate it—
It shall be
(*To Octavius*)
Did you speak, sir?
OCTAVIUS.
N-Not a squeak, sir
BARRETT.
Now attend to me
You'll do in all things precisely as
I say
And when I give an order, you will
Instantly obey

(BARRETT *takes off his smoking-jacket.* OCTAVIUS *catches it and lays it on the seat down* R. CHARLES *goes off up* L *and returns with Barrett's coat*)

Stay or go—as I wish it
Quick or slow—as I wish it
Yes, or no, contradict it
If you can
GEORGE.
Who, sir? Me, sir?
I agree, sir.

(BARRETT *puts on his coat, helped by* CHARLES)

BARRETT *and* GEORGE (*singing together*)
I'm ⎱
You're ⎰ the Master man
THE BROTHERS.
Right is wrong
BARRETT.
If I state it
THE BROTHERS.
Wrong is right if you state it
BARRETT.
Right or wrong—I dictate it
Is that plain?
THE BROTHERS.
Here and now, sir
We avow, sir
You're the master brain

(BARRETT *crosses* R *towards Septimus.* SEPTIMUS *rises*)

True is false
BARRETT.
If I swear it
THE BROTHERS.
False is true if you swear it
BARRETT.
True or false I declare it
Is my choice
THE BROTHERS.
Let us say, sir, right away, sir
You're the master voice.

(BARRETT *crosses* L. GEORGE *gives him his cigar-case from the mantelpiece.* ALFRED *exits up* L *and returns with Barrett's overcoat*)

BARRETT.
Here, as it was, in the glory that was Rome
THE BROTHERS.
Parental authority is paramount at home
BARRETT.
High is high

THE BROTHERS.
>As the sky, sir

BARRETT.
>Low is low

THE BROTHERS.
>That we know, sir

BARRETT.
>High is low, low is high, if that's my will

(ALFRED *helps* BARRETT *to put on his overcoat*)

THE BROTHERS.
>None can doubt you
>Dare to flout you
>You're the master still

(SEPTIMUS *gets Barrett's gloves from up* C)

BARRETT.
>You'll do in all things
>Whatever I may feel
>And when I crack the whip, my friends
>You'll promptly come to heel.

(BARRETT *takes his gloves from Septimus.* OCTAVIUS *brings Barrett's hat and stick from up* C)

THE BROTHERS.
>We shall obey your least command

BARRETT.
>Might is right

THE BROTHERS.
>You are right, sir

BARRETT.
>Law is law

THE BROTHERS.
>That is sure, sir
>Might is law, law is might
>You've made it clear

BARRETT.
>You don't challenge it?

THE BROTHERS.
>What son would dare to?

BARRETT.
>Query it?

(BARRETT *takes his hat and stick from* OCTAVIUS *and moves upstage*)

THE BROTHERS.
>We wouldn't care to question it
>For you're the master
>There's no doubt about who's master

BARRETT.   THE BROTHERS.
  I'm the master here   You're the master here
(ALFRED *goes to the front door and opens it*)
                           You're the master here!

BARRETT *exits through the front door and* ALFRED *closes it, as the* LIGHTS *fade to a* BLACK-OUT.

SCENE 3

Cremorne Gardens, Chelsea. Evening

A wooded park near London river, to which on warm summer nights fashionable and less fashionable society repairs to eat, drink, dance and dally among the trees. There are winkle and whelk stalls, a bar, coffee urns, and music playing for the dancers.

CREMORNE QUADRILLE   No. 22

When the LIGHTS *come up, a fancy dress ball is in full progress.* BROWNING *is sitting writing* L *of the table* RC, *and guests are dancing the Lancers. In the last figure of the dance,* BELLA, BEVAN, DR CHAMBERS *and a* LADY *are dancing down* C. *The music is that of "The Moon in my Pocket". A* SANDWICH-BOARD MAN *enters down* L. *The music continues during the first part of the dialogue.*

SANDWICH-BOARD MAN. Down with tyranny! Death to the oppressors! All men are tyrants! (*To Chambers*) Prepare to meet thy doom.

CHAMBERS (*dancing with Bella*) Yes, yes, not now, my dear fellow.

  (MACREADY, *who is not dancing, stalks disdainfully through the crowd*)

SANDWICH-BOARD MAN. All men are tyrants and oppressors!

CHAMBERS. Do go away—this is a gala occasion, you know. His Royal Highness Prince Albert's birthday.

  (MACREADY *moves* L *of the Sandwich-board Man*)

SANDWICH-BOARD MAN. Royalty is no exception. (*To Macready*) Prepare to meet thy doom.

MACREADY. Sir, I met it the day I entered the theatrical profession.

SANDWICH-BOARD MAN. The theatre—doomed!

  (*A* POLICEMAN *takes the Sandwich-board Man upstage. The dance finishes, with the company in the following positions:* BROWNING *seated* L *of the* RC *table,* BELLA *downstage* L *of him,* BEVAN *up* L *of Bella,* CHAMBERS *down* C, LADY MARY *upstage* L *of Chambers,* MACREADY L)

BELLA. Thank you, Dr Chambers. I did enjoy that! What a gorgeous whythm! I do adore music, don't you, Mr Macweady?

MACREADY. Madam, I detest all fiddlers and music-masters. They distract the public from the legitimate stage.

LADY MARY (*an attractive socialite*) Oh, William, don't be such a boor.

MACREADY. Scrapers and wire-thumpers, bellow-blowers and throat-crackers. An abomination, the lot of them.

LADY MARY. How else would you celebrate the Prince Consort's birthday?

MACREADY. Frankly, madam, I wouldn't.

BELLA. Misanthwopist!

LADY MARY. Yes, Robert Browning would put you to shame.

BELLA. Wobert Bwowning! Is *he* here?

LADY MARY. Over there—at that table.

BELLA (*turning to see Browning*) Oh! What is he witing? A poem or a play?

LADY MARY. I'm not sure. It might be a play.

MACREADY. In that case, if you'll excuse me . . . (*He moves upstage*)

BELLA (*moving to Browning*) Mr Browning, do forgive me—but I adore your poetwy. "Oh, to be in England, now it's March". Do wead it to us.

BROWNING. It's not finished yet.

BELLA. Mawy, won't you persuade him? (*She moves above the table to R of it*)

LADY MARY. Read it, Robert.

BROWNING. It's only a rough draft.

LADY MARY. Never mind, read it.

BELLA. Please.

(*Reluctantly,* BROWNING *starts to read, then to sing*)

"ESCAPE ME NEVER"

No. 23

BROWNING (*spoken*)
    Escape me never
    Beloved
    While I am I—
    (*Singing*)
        and you are you
    So long as earth contains us two

(*The* CROWD *gradually becomes silent, moving downstage to form a group as* BROWNING *sweeps into the song with deep feeling*)

    While one eludes, must the other pursue
    Forever, Beloved
    Forever

Escape me never
Beloved
While you are you and I am I
While there is ocean, while there is sky
Though it be not till the day we die
We'll be together
Escape me never
Forever and aye

CROWD. Escape me never
Beloved
While I am I and you are you
So long as earth contains us two
While one eludes, must the other pursue
Forever, beloved
Forever.

BROWNING.
Escape me never
Beloved
The earth divides. Beyond the hill
The land is frozen, the seas are still
But hope lives on and eternally will
We'll be together
Escape me never

CROWD. Forever and aye
Escape me never
Beloved
While you are you and I am I
While there is ocean, while there is sky

BROWNING.
Though it be not till the day we die

BROWNING and CROWD (*singing together*)
We'll be together
Escape me never
Forever and aye

LADY MARY. What a sad little piece.

BELLA. But wildly womantic. Who is she, Mr Bwowning?

BROWNING (*lightly*) No one you know. (*He smiles briefly*) No one I know—now.

(*In the distance fireworks shoot brilliantly up into the night and burst their cluster across the sky*)

(*Rising*) Come on, let's go down to the water and cheer Albert the Good on his natal day.

(*More fireworks shower upwards. The* CROWD *starts to stream out up* L. BROWNING *moves upstage, then turns* C, *with* LADY MARY *on his* L *and* BELLA *on his* R)

(*Roaring up at the night*)
Hello, you sacristan, show us a light there!

Down it drops, fine like a rocket.
What, you want, do you, to come unawares,
Sweeping the Church up for first morning prayers,
And find a poor devil has ended his cares
At the foot of your rotten-runged rat-ridden stairs
Do I carry the moon in my pocket?
(*To Lady Mary*) Do you like that better?
LADY MARY. Yes.
BELLA. But what does it mean?
BROWNING. I've no idea.

(*More fireworks explode.* BELLA, LADY MARY *and* BROWNING *exit up* L *with most of the* CROWD. SURTEES COOK, *the* FELLOW OFFICER *and a small* GROUP *remain at the winkle stall down* L. *As the stage empties,* HENRIETTA, *cloaked and hooded, hurries in up* R. *She looks furtively this way and that, spies Cook at the whelk stall, and whispers to the* FELLOW OFFICER)

FELLOW OFFICER (*to Cook*) Er, Captain. There's a certain young lady wants to speak to a certain "officer" privately.
COOK. Oh! In that case, I'll leave you alone. (*He starts to exit down* L)
HENRIETTA. Oh, don't be an ass, it's me. (*She throws back her hood*)
COOK. Good Lord, hello, hello. (*He moves to her,* C)

(*With a broad grin the* FELLOW OFFICER *exits up* L. *The remaining* CROWD *drift away after him*)

HENRIETTA (*urgently*) I had to see you—just once more.
COOK. So did I. By Jove.
HENRIETTA. Good-bye. (*She moves up* R)
COOK. Good-bye. Wait! Henrietta! Where are you going?
HENRIETTA (*moving down to* R *of Cook*) To the ends of the earth—Rookham or Bookham or something ghastly. Father's taken a dungeon there. We're all going to be buried alive.
COOK. You mean, you're leaving Wimpole Street?
HENRIETTA. For ever!
COOK. When?
HENRIETTA. Tuesday.
COOK. Good Lord! Disaster!
HENRIETTA. It's worse than that. Have you ever tried hugging a bull, or cuddling a cow, or kissing a pig?
COOK. Darling, I'm in the Guards. I say, what's this about?
HENRIETTA (*desperately*) My life! Nothing but bulls and cows and pigs—that's what it's going to be from now on—and never a soul for miles and miles! And just when I'd found the perfect man!
COOK (*upset*) Really? Anyone I know?

HENRIETTA. Oh, for Heaven's sake, who do you think?

COOK. I say, that's frightfully decent of you, and, of course, you know how I feel about you—absolutely worship the ground you glide over.

HENRIETTA. I know—you mustn't.

COOK. I can't seem to help myself.

HENRIETTA. You must try, Surtees. We must both try extremely hard.

"HATE ME, PLEASE"

No. 24

(*singing*)
Hate me, please
You'd make me very happy if you'd
Hate me, please
I really would be grateful if you'd
Chide me, cheat me
Cut my heart in half
Take the thing and break the thing
And give a merry laugh, ho—ho!
Deceive me, do
Be absolutely beastly
I'll be happy to
Be beastly back to you
There's just a slender chance
Our beautiful romance
Would not survive
If you would bury me alive

COOK (*spoken*) Henrietta!

HENRIETTA.
Stop! Don't fondle me or fête me
Things aren't going smoothly lately
Darling, if you love me blindly
Kindly hate me, please.

(*The* MUSIC *continues*)

COOK (*spoken*) I don't know how to.

HENRIETTA (*spoken*) We've got to get over each other—and you've got to help me to hate you.

COOK. You mean, hate each other?

HENRIETTA. Yes.

COOK. Me hate you?

HENRIETTA. Yes.

COOK. And you hate me?

HENRIETTA. Yes.

COOK. When?

HENRIETTA. Now!

Cook. Right! (*Singing*)
>Hate me, please
>I'd be a happy chappie if you'd
>Hate me, please
>I'd take it as a favour if you'd
>Loathe me, leave me,
>Tear my heart in two
>Carve it up and halve it up
>And serve it to the zoo.

Henrietta (*spoken*) You've got it.

Cook.   Cut my hair
>Be deadly as Delilah and
>I hereby swear
>Your scalp will be as bare
>There's just an outside chance
>This wonderful romance
>Would cease to grow
>Were each the other's Figaro.

Cook *and* Henrietta (*singing together*)
>Love, don't fondle or fête me

Henrietta.
>Be like Father and berate me

Cook.   Clearly, if you love me dearly
>You must hate me, please.

Henrietta.
>You only to love me
>You only to care
>Your smile in the morning

Cook.   Your step on the stair.

Henrietta (*spoken*) No! (*Singing*)
>Hate me, please
>I'd be in seventh heaven if you'd

Cook *and* Henrietta (*singing together*)
>Hate me, please

Cook.   It really would oblige me if you'd
>Shun me

Henrietta.
>Shock me,

Cook.   Tear my heart in twain

Henrietta.
>Jump on it and stamp on it
>And jump on it again.

Cook.   Wound me, wing me
>Stab me, sting me,

Henrietta.
>Something's to be flung

Cook.   Then fling me
>Someone's to be clung to?

Henrietta.
    Cling me!
Cook.   You only to love me
Henrietta (*spoken*) *No!*
Cook (*spoken*) Sorry.
Cook *and* Henrietta (*singing together*)
    Bully, bait me
    Decimate me
    Oh, my best beloved, hate me,
    On my knees I beg you,
    Hate me, please!
Henrietta (*melting; spoken*) Sur*tees* . . .
    (*They go into a passionate embrace*)
Good-bye! (*She moves up* R)
Cook (*following*) What do you mean, good-bye? I'm not
letting you go without a fight.
Henrietta. You can't fight Father. He always wins. Good-bye
forever!

    (*There is a last, short burst of fireworks.* Henrietta *exits up* R.
Browning *and* Chambers *enter up* L *and come down* C, Chambers
to R. *The* Crowd *follows.* Cook *moves* L *of Browning*)

Cook. I say, Browning, what the devil are we going to do?
The Barretts are leaving town.
Browning. What?!
Cook. He's bundling them off to the country.
Browning. All of them?
Cook. Lock, stock and Henrietta.
Browning. A holiday?
Cook. No, for life.
Chambers. That man!
Cook. We've got to stop it.
Browning. Not so easy.
Cook. Why don't they just refuse to go? Dash it, they're
grown up, they've got minds of their own, haven't they?
Browning. No. They haven't. That's just the trouble.

"UNDER A SPELL"

No.
25

(*Singing*)   They're under a spell
    Completely bewitched
    Their brains have been taken to pieces
    And twisted and twiddled and twitched
    They're under a drug
    The drug is a man
    To make them his puppets and slaves
    Is the body and soul of his plan
    To think for yourself
    Is never allowed

Their wits have been taken to pieces
And shattered and battered and cowed
It's a joy to be grim
It's a crime to be glad
A matter of weeks and
He'll have them besotted and totally mad.

CHAMBERS (*spoken*) The man's a monster.

COOK. A despot.

CHAMBERS. Inhuman.

BROWNING. A tyrant.

SANDWICH-BOARD MAN. All men are tyrants!

A POOR MAN. No! All men are slaves!

BROWNING (*singing*)
The world is as strong
As the strength of humanity's will to be free
But then comes along
A bully who bellows:
"The world is for me".

CROWD (*shouting*) Yes!

BROWNING.
He spreads it abroad
That freedom's a lie

COOK. You hear his appeal
And you're under his heel
In the wink of an eye

BROWNING.
You long for release

COOK. But now it's too late

BROWNING.
He's swallowed you whole
And your body and soul
Are the slave of the state.

COOK. Down with tyranny! Down with tyranny!

CROWD.
Up with freedom!

COOK. Down with tyranny! Up with liberty!

CROWD.
Rouse 'em! Lead 'em!

SANDWICH-BOARD MAN.
Wherever it rears its ugly head
Wherever it's written or sung or said
Take it, shatter it
Break it, batter it,

COOK. Strike it dead!

(*Shouts of "Hurrah!", etc.*)

BROWNING.
Down with tyranny! Down with tyranny!

CROWD.
    Up with freedom!
BROWNING.
    Down with tyranny! Up with liberty!
CROWD.
    Fight 'em! Bleed 'em!
BROWNING.
    Whatever its colour or shape or race
    Wherever it's found a resting-place,
CROWD.
    Storm it, strangle it,
    Smite it, mangle it,
BROWNING and CROWD (singing together)
    Smash its face!

BROWNING.	CROWD.
(singing together)	
They're under a spell	Down with tyranny!
Completely bewitched	Up with liberty!
Their brains have been	
taken to pieces	Down with tyranny!
And twisted and twiddled and	
twitched	Down with tyranny!

SANDWICH-BOARD MAN.

(singing together)	
Why don't they resist?	Up with liberty!
Why can't they rebel?	Down with tyranny!

BROWNING.

(singing together)	
It's easy to say	Up with liberty!
But the devil's to pay	Down with tyranny!
They're tolling the bell	Up
For your soul is in hell	with liberty!
When you're under a spell	

ELEGANT CROWD.
    Law and order!
ROUGH CROWD.
    Down with tyranny!
ELEGANT CROWD.
    Starve them, quell them!
ROUGH CROWD.
    Flog them, fell them!
ELEGANT CROWD.
    Bind them, beat them!
ROUGH CROWD.
    Swine, defeat them!
ALL.   Set us free of the spell!

    (THE SPELL BALLET is danced. As it reaches the climax,
BROWNING suddenly breaks in)

BROWNING (*spoken*)
              Break the gates of the mind,
              And you'll suddenly find—
(*Singing*)   That you've broken the spell!

              BLACK-OUT

              SCENE CHANGE MUSIC   No.
              (Reprise from L)   25

              SCENE 4

         The Hall of Number Fifty Wimpole Street

Everywhere are signs of imminent departure. The furniture is partly gone and what remains is shrouded in dust-sheets. There is an open trunk on the floor C.

When the LIGHTS *come up,* OCTAVIUS *is discovered sitting on the seat down* L, ALFRED *is standing down* R, GEORGE *by the french windows* R, HENRIETTA *sitting on the floor down* L *of the trunk* C, CHARLES *sitting on the seat above the fire* L, HENRY *standing up* R, SEPTIMUS L *of the trunk* C. ARABEL *enters downstairs.*

"THE GIRLS THAT BOYS DREAM ABOUT"   No.
                                     26

OCTAVIUS. Do you think London will miss us when we're g-gone?
ALFRED. The girls will.
GEORGE (*moving above the trunk* C) Ah yes. The girls.

(ARABEL *sits on the floor above Henrietta*)

HENRIETTA. Girls? But you're not allowed girls.
CHARLES. We can dream, can't we?
GEORGE. We always have.
HENRY (*sitting on the seat up* R) Dear Emily.
SEPTIMUS (*closing the lid of the trunk and sitting on it*) Dear Julia.
ALFRED (*moving* R *of the trunk*) Dear Marie-Louise.
OCTAVIUS. M-Marie-Louise? Is she beautiful?
ALFRED. No, just female!
THE BROTHERS (*singing*)
              The girls that boys dream about
              May not have poise
              The girls that boys dream about
              Cuddle their toys
              But the girls that boys dream about
              Dream about boys

(HENRIETTA *rises and sits* L *on the stool down* L)

              Dream about
              Dream about
              Boys.

(ARABEL *moves* R *of Henrietta and sits*)
> The girls that boys dream about
> May have their fads
> The girls that boys dream about
> Live with their dads
> But the girls that boys dream about
> Dream about lads
> Dream about
> Dream about
> Lads.

ARABEL *and* HENRIETTA (*singing together*)
> The boys that girls dream about
> Needn't be earls
> The boys that girls dream about
> Needn't buy pearls
> If the boys that girls dream about
> Dream about girls
> Dream about
> Dream about
> Girls.

BROTHERS.
> The girls that we hunger for
> Don't make a fuss

ARABEL *and* HENRIETTA.
> If the boys that we hunger for
> Blow us a buss

BROTHERS *and* SISTERS (*singing together*)
> For the ones that we hunger for
> Hunger for us
> Dream about
> Dream about
> Us.

(WILSON *enters up* C, *moves to the stairs and pauses half-way up them*)
> The clock ticks on
> And love goes by

ARABEL *and* HENRIETTA.
> But hope stays strong

(HENRY *moves to* R *of Charles.* OCTAVIUS *rises, moves* L *of Henrietta and takes her hand*)
> And still we wonder and sigh

HENRIETTA.
> Will the day a girl dreams about

(WILSON *comes down and stands down* L *of the trunk* C)
> Ever come true?

ARABEL.   With your friends and relations
            In pew after pew
HENRIETTA.
            And the boy that you've waited for
            Waiting for you.
HENRIETTA *and* ARABEL.
            Waiting for
            Waiting for
            You.
WILSON.   The clock ticks on
            The years go by
            And when you're old
            You'll look back with a sigh
THE SISTERS.
            For the days that are over
            The bells that were rung
WILSON.   The dances you danced
            And the songs you have sung
THE BROTHERS.
            But the girls that boys dream about
            Always stay young
ALL.   Always stay
            Always stay
            Young
            In the mem'ry
            Touchingly, timelessly
            Young.

GEORGE *kisses* WILSON. SEPTIMUS *and* ALFRED *move the trunk upstage.* BROWNING *enters through the french windows* R *and runs off up the stairs.* CHARLES, ARABEL, HENRY *and* OCTAVIUS *move upstage.* COOK *appears at the french windows.* WILSON *sees him and goes to Henrietta.* HENRIETTA *runs across to* COOK *and they exit through the french windows.* WILSON *goes upstage as—*

the LIGHTS *fade*

SCENE CHANGE MUSIC   No. 27

SCENE 5

Elizabeth's room. Night

When the LIGHTS *come up,* ELIZABETH, *in a negligee, is standing at the open window* L, *tense. There is a knock at the door.* ELIZABETH *turns.* BROWNING *strides in to* C. *He stares at her, seeing her on her feet.* ELIZABETH *runs to him, and they meet and embrace down* C. *He smothers her with kisses, breaks, holds her at arm's length.*

BROWNING (*with wonder and joy*) Want to be well and it's done! You've won!

ELIZABETH. Robert, you shouldn't have come . . .

BROWNING. I should never have stayed away—and when I saw you at that window, do you think an earthquake could stop me?

ELIZABETH. Ssh! Not so loud.

BROWNING. Where is he?

ELIZABETH. Out at White's, but if he hears you came . . .

BROWNING (*throwing his cloak on the pouffe and moving to the window* L) Let him. I'd like to smash every casement of this infernal house and shout to the world—(*flinging the curtains open*)—"I love Elizabeth Barrett!" But I'll spare your blushes until we're married—which, by the way, we must be at once.

ELIZABETH. Do you know what you're saying?

BROWNING. Yes, and I'll repeat it. We must be married at once. Secretly, if you will, but at once. Now then . . .

ELIZABETH. I can't marry you, Robert—secretly or openly.

BROWNING. You'll marry me if I have to carry you screaming to the altar. Do you think I'm going to be elbowed out of your life by a man whom I no longer believe to be sane? You don't know me. (*He crosses up* R *to the bookcase*)

ELIZABETH. Robert—it's not just Father who stands between us—it's I.

BROWNING (*moving to the desk and opening a Baedeker*) Is that a Baedeker?

ELIZABETH. Oh, I know I'm well now, but there's no guarantee for the future.

BROWNING (*studying the Baedeker*) On the whole I think this is our best plan of campaign. The family, I gather, move to their country prison next week—

(ELIZABETH *moves to the window*)

—so we should leave for the Continent not later than Saturday, if there's a suitable ferry . . .

ELIZABETH. It's impossible . . .

BROWNING. Yes, here we are—the cross-channel ferry sails from Southampton—(*writing a note*)—on Saturday evenings at nine o'clock. That means we must catch the five o'clock express from Vauxhall. It arrives at Southampton at eight.

ELIZABETH (*moving to the chair* L *of the table* C *and sitting*) This is utterly out of the question.

BROWNING. Of course, you can't travel without a maid. Do you think Wilson would come to Italy with us?

ELIZABETH. Italy?

BROWNING. Where else? The best way to elope is to tell no one at all, but we'll have to trust Wilson. (*Crossing upstage to* L *of Elizabeth*) I'll arrange for a doctor to meet us at the other end. Quite unnecessary, but with something so precious I'm taking no chances. (*He gives Elizabeth the note*) Now, will you speak to Wilson or shall I? It must be settled at once.

ELIZABETH. And I always believed Father was the most over-bearing man in the world.

BROWNING (*sitting at the* R *end of the sofa*) And yet you've known me for some time now. You've made me so completely happy, I've never stopped to wonder if you were happy too. (*He rises*) Total selfishness—from the first moment I walked through that door and you threw all those pills at me. About Saturday—where shall we meet?

ELIZABETH. I keep telling you, it's impossible.

BROWNING. And I tell you nothing is impossible if you have the will—(*kneeling* L *of her*)—your own will. You're leaving this cage on Saturday. Nothing can stop us.

ELIZABETH. I wish you were right.

BROWNING. I'm always right. Did nobody tell you?

(ELIZABETH *rises and moves below the sofa*)

Saturday. You will come?

(ELIZABETH *turns away, tense, uncertain*)

(*Rising and turning her towards him*) Elizabeth!

ELIZABETH. I—I can't decide now. I must have time.

BROWNING. Time is short.

ELIZABETH. Yes, I know, but—I'll send you a note. Twenty-four hours—give me twenty-four hours.

BROWNING. I want to give you the rest of my life.

(*They kiss passionately, then* BROWNING *picks up his cloak from the pouffe*)

ELIZABETH. I'll send you a note—one way or the other.

BROWNING (*turning to her*) One way . . .

ELIZABETH. Yes—or good-bye.

(*The door opens.* BARRETT *enters and moves above the table* C. ELIZABETH *conceals the note*)

BARRETT (*at length*) I was under the impression that you'd been forbidden this house.

BROWNING (*moving* R *of Barrett; deliberately*) I shan't come here again.

(BROWNING *looks steadily at Elizabeth, then exits up* C)

BARRETT. So this is why you wished me not to visit you late at night!

ELIZABETH. No, Papa.

BARRETT. How long has this deceit been going on? How often has he been here behind my back?

ELIZABETH. Mr Browning has not been here at all, until tonight.

BARRETT (*moving to Elizabeth*) You expect me to believe that?
ELIZABETH. It's the truth.
BARRETT. Is he your lover? (*Seizing her hands and shouting*)
Answer me!
ELIZABETH. If you mean, do we love each other—yes. We do.

(BARRETT *forces her to her knees and throws her against the sofa. Then he moves above the sofa*)

BARRETT (*after a pause*) You will fetch your Bible, you will place your hand upon it, and you will give me your solemn oath that you will neither see nor communicate with this man again.
ELIZABETH. No.
BARRETT. You refuse?
ELIZABETH. I love him, Father.
BARRETT. *LOVE!* You ignorant little fool. What do *you* know of love? It's time a little reality were brought into your dream of life!

"WHAT THE WORLD CALLS LOVE"   No. 28

(*Speaking in time*)
　　　　What the world calls love
　　　　Is a purely passing passion
　　　　An irrational infection of the brain
(*Singing*)　What the world calls love
　　　　Is pain
　　　　What the world calls love
　　　　Is a momentary gladness
　　　　Then the madness and the agony begin
　　　　What the world calls love
　　　　Is sin.
　　　　(*He moves* L *of Elizabeth*)
　　　　Love they beg
　　　　Until they're hoarse
　　　　(*Taking her hands*)
　　　　Love is deg-
　　　　radation and remorse
　　　　What the world calls love
　　　　Isn't sweetness, isn't kindness
　　　　But a blindness that the simple see too late
　　　　What the world calls love
　　　　I hate
　　　　(*He pulls her to her feet*)
　　　　I tell you
　　　　Love's a game for fools to trust
　　　　Love is just another name for lust
　　　　(*He throws her towards* C)
　　　　What the world calls love
　　　　Is a torment and a folly

And this melancholy, miserable state
That the sinful, wilful
World calls love
I—
(*Spoken*)
—abominate!

(BARRETT *turns down* L *with his back to Elizabeth*)

ELIZABETH. Your ideas of love—like your ideas of right and justice and duty are wrong—all wrong!

"WOMAN AND MAN"

No.
28a

(*Singing*) Woman and man were meant for each other
Man as her husband, man as her lover
Woman as wife and daughter and mother
Woman and man are meant for each other.

That was the end from the beginning
Partner and friend, losing or winning
Man and his mate, saintly or sinning
Woman and man from the very beginning.

Dark is the night and wild is the weather
Woman and man draw closer together
Cynics can laugh, but whatever they say
Love is the start and the heart and the
hope of the day.

Woman and man were meant for each other
Man as her husband, man as her lover
Woman as wife and daughter and mother
Woman and man are meant for each other.

(*She moves above the chair* L *of the table* C)
Dark is the night and wild is the weather
Woman and man draw closer together
Cynics can laugh and say love is a lie
But for woman and man
Love is surely forever and aye.

BARRETT (*moving* L *of Elizabeth*) If there were a vestige of truth in what you say, my whole life would be a mockery. But how can you, in your innocence, your ignorance, know what it means to have a man touch you, tear you, crush you until you're sick with fear and pain. I tell you, *that* is love. *That* is marriage.

ELIZABETH (*moving below the sofa and sitting*) I don't believe you. I won't listen to you. (*She puts her hands over her ears*)

(BARRETT *moves* R *of Elizabeth*)

BARRETT. Take your hands from your face. Look at me! Look at me, I say! (*He takes her hands and turns her to him*) I have told you the truth. Not only of other men. Of all men. Of myself. (*He releases her*)

ELIZABETH. Are you saying your love for Mama was like that?

BARRETT. My love for your mother *was* love. You were born of it. You and Edward. But long before the others came, there was nothing left, nothing, but the look of fear on your mother's face whenever I touched her.

ELIZABETH. Fear? All those children were born of . . . It's horrible! Horrible! (*She turns from him*)

BARRETT. Now do you understand me? I crushed this vileness in my own nature and as long as I live I will keep it from those it is my duty to protect and care for. Above all, from you. (*Sitting beside her*) Listen, my child, listen! Soon we shall have left this house, and in our new home we shall grow closer together, you and I. There will be nothing and no one to come between us. My dear, my darling, the only happiness I shall ever know is yours to give or take. You must look up to me, depend on me, lean on me, share your thoughts with me, your hopes, your fears, your prayers. (*He embraces her*) My child, my child, my own dear girl, I want all your heart and all your soul and . . . (*His arms are tightly round her, his face close to hers*)

ELIZABETH (*turning away*) No! Let me go! Let me go!

BARRETT. Forgive me. (*He releases her and rises*) Rest now, you must rest. (*He moves above the sofa*) Tonight I shall pray alone. Pray that you may come to understand your father's love for you—(*He stops, almost breaking down*)—and his *need* of you. (*He crosses to the door* R, *then turns*) Elizabeth—"Lovers grow cold, men learn to hate their wives, and only parents' love can last our lives". Do you know who wrote that?

(ELIZABETH *looks up at him*)

Robert Browning.

BARRETT *exits* R. *The door closes.* ELIZABETH *stares into space, shaken, uncertain, afraid, as—*

the LIGHTS *fade*

SCENE CHANGE MUSIC

No.
28b

SCENE 6

A terrace outside Browning's study. Evening

When the LIGHTS *come up,* EVANS *is discovered standing by a small
table down* L. BROWNING *enters through a french window* RC *and
moves* C.

"FRUSTRATION"   No.
29

BROWNING (*speaking over the music, his nerves at breaking point*)
What time is it? Just gone six. Too late for another post tonight.
(*He paces*)
EVANS. It may come by hand, sir. Cheer up, sir! No news is
good news.
BROWNING. Not necessarily. In any case—either way—good
or bad . . .
(*Singing*)
    I would infinitely rather know the worst
    Oh, I love her—I have loved her from the first
    But the tension, the frustration
    The eternal vacillation
    If she doesn't make her mind up
    I shall burst!
EVANS (*spoken*) She's a woman, sir.
BROWNING (*singing*)
    I'm aware that she's a woman. That is fine
    And she's much more than a woman: she's divine

    (EVANS *picks up a tray from the table*)

    She's a goddess from the heavens
    But I tell you frankly, Evans
    While she tries to make her mind up
    I'm losing mine!
EVANS (*moving to the french windows; spoken*) Don't say that, sir.

    (EVANS *exits.* BROWNING *moves to the chair* L *and puts one knee
on it*)

BROWNING (*singing*)
    Here I hang
    Like a felon on a rope
    Swinging wildly to and fro
    Between despondency and hope
    Now I'm clear
    What they mean by "love is blind"
    They mean no one but God can gauge
    The workings of the female mind

(*He sits in the chair*)
By my nature I am timid, I am meek
One who's more inclined to whisper than to speak
But although I dearly love her
(*Rising*)
By the firmament above her
If she won't make a decision

(Evans *enters and stands* R *of the french window*)

I shall shriek!
Evans (*spoken*) Relax, sir.
Browning (*crossing down* R; *spoken*) How can I? (*Singing*)
One second I'm as high as the hills
(*He crosses down* L *to above the table*)
The next I'm as low as the plains
Is it stay? Is it go?
Is it yes? Is it no?
Does she want me to blow out my brains?
Evans (*taking a pace downstage*) Be patient, sir.
Browning.
I've been patient!—
(*Moving* C)
                    God, the patience that I've showed!
Why, a saint who'd been as patient would have glowed!
If this goes on any longer—
Every hour my need grows stronger—
We had better face it, Evans,
I'll explode!

Up I'll go
In a holocaust of heat
There'll be little bits of Browning
Strewn all over Wimpole Street
Tears she'll shed
For the man she claims she loves
But all that's left of Browning
Will be a pair of yellow gloves.

(*There is a rat-a-tat on the front door.* Browning *and* Evans *both move to the french window.* Evans *gets there first, and exits.* Browning *moves* L *and sits. He picks up a book to read—after a moment realizes it is upside down and turns it round, then puts it on the table.* Evans *enters with a letter.* Browning *rises to* C *and opens it.* Evans *exits. The music continues throughout*)

(*Singing; suddenly delirious with happiness*)
Anyone who doubts a woman should be shot!
I deserve to be beheaded on the spot!

Who said women were like sponges?
When she plunges, woman plunges
She's the wonder of the world—
And man is not!

BLACK-OUT

The music continues through to—

SCENE 7

Vauxhall Station

Part of a train is drawn up at a platform L

As the LIGHTS *come up an announcement through a megaphone is heard:
"The five o'clock boat train for Southampton is now standing at
Number Two Platform. The Southampton boat train is now waiting
at Platform Number Two." There are* PASSERS-BY, *and waiting*
PASSENGERS. WILSON *enters* R *and comes down* C. *She is harassed,
tense and nervous.*

REPRISE—"FRUSTRATION"

No.
29a

WILSON (*singing*)
Why's a station even blacker than a fog?
Why is life a rush and not a gentle jog?
Had a good post, nicely suited,
Then I'm suddenly uprooted
Now I've been and gone and lost
The bloody dog!

(WILSON *moves up* R, *shouting "Flush! Flush!"* COOK *enters up*
L *and moves down* C. *He is in mufti, and strides nervously up and
down*)

COOK (*singing*)
Now I've left the Army for the civvy side
Will my Henrietta look at me with pride?
Will she hug me? Will she huff me?
When she sees her man in mufti
Will she even know for sure
It's me inside?

(COOK *moves up* L. WILSON *comes down* RC)

WILSON. Hound of Hell!
Does he want to watch me die?
COOK (*moving down* LC)
Supposing what attracted her
Was just my uniform, not I?

(WILSON *moves down* R)

Will she care
Now that I'm a city gent?
WILSON (*moving* R *of Cook*)
Must find the brute before he floods
Half Middlesex and all of Kent
(*She moves to a group of passengers* R)
Anybody seen a spaniel on the spree?
COOK (*moving to a group of passengers* L)
Got to try and make a spot of l.s.d.

(WILSON *and* COOK *move* C)

WILSON. He's a cocker
COOK. Must support her
WILSON. He's a shocker!

(*A* PORTER *crosses upstage from* L *to* R *with mailbags*)

COOK. Who is?
WILSON. Porter!
WILSON *and* COOK (*singing to each other*)
If you think that you've got problems—
Look at me! Look at me! Look at me!
Look at me! Look at me!

(WILSON *and* COOK *curtsy and bow to each other.* WILSON *then exits down* L. BROWNING *enters up* R *and moves to* R *of Cook.* EVANS *enters up* R *and moves up* C, *with luggage*)

MELOS

No.
29b

BROWNING (*to Cook*) Is she here?
COOK. Who? Henrietta?
BROWNING. No, Elizabeth.
COOK. No.
BROWNING. She's cutting it fine.

(BROWNING *moves up* L, COOK *down* R)

COOK. She's a woman.
BROWNING. I'm aware of that.
EVANS. All present and correct, sir.
BROWNING (*nervously, looking off* R) Come on, come on, come *on*.
(*He crosses down* R)

(COOK *crosses* L. EVANS *moves down* LC)

EVANS. She's a woman, sir. (*He takes a hatbox from Browning and moves upstage*)
BROWNING. Evans, if anyone else makes that observation I shall . . .
COOK (*moving to Browning*) Don't worry. Henrietta will see that she gets here. Most remarkable girl, Henrietta. I don't know whether you've noticed.

BROWNING (*crossing* L) No, I haven't.
COOK. Oh.

(ELIZABETH *enters* R *and meets* BROWNING C. *The* MELOS *stops.* HENRIETTA *follows Elizabeth and meets* COOK R)

ELIZABETH. Robert!
BROWNING. Thank heaven!

(ELIZABETH *and* BROWNING *embrace*)

I was afraid there'd been an accident.
ELIZABETH. There has. Wilson has lost the dog.
BROWNING. Good Lord!
ELIZABETH. Is there another train tonight?
BROWNING. Nothing that will connect with the ferry.
ELIZABETH. Then we'll just have to go without him, that's all.
(*She moves* R)
BROWNING. I suppose we could stay overnight.
ELIZABETH (*at once*) No! I shan't feel safe till we're out of London.
BROWNING. Elizabeth—you've nothing to fear.
ELIZABETH (*moving* L *of Browning*) I know—but fear has become a habit. I shan't feel absolutely safe till the train pulls into Florence station.

(WILSON *enters down* L *carrying* FLUSH *and moves to Elizabeth*)

WILSON. Here he is, the little b-eauty.
ELIZABETH. Where have you been, you bad dog?

(WILSON *puts Flush in the train. A guard's whistle sounds off stage*)

HENRIETTA. You'd better get in, Ba.

(*They all move towards the train*)

ELIZABETH. Yes. Good-bye, my darling. I'll write. I'll never stop writing.

(ELIZABETH *and* HENRIETTA *embrace emotionally*)

(*Turning to Cook*) Take good care of her.
COOK. Absolutely. Never fear. Never was such a girl, y'know
—Henrietta, I mean . . .
HENRIETTA (*happily*) Oh, for Heaven's sake!

(*As* ELIZABETH *steps to the carriage door, which* BROWNING *holds open for her, there is a sudden commotion off up* R. ARABEL *rushes on, followed by a* TICKET COLLECTOR *who stops her at the barrier* C)

MELOS   No.
                               29c

TICKET COLLECTOR. Here, miss! Wait! Where's your ticket?
ARABEL (*extremely agitated*) I'm not travelling! I'm not
travelling! Let me go on!
TICKET COLLECTOR. You must have a ticket to go on the
platform.
ARABEL. I haven't time! Please! You must let me go on!
Let me pass!

(BROWNING *goes to the* TICKET COLLECTOR *and gives him a
coin.* ARABEL *runs to* ELIZABETH *and they come down* LC)

(*Hysterically*) Oh, Ba, I *didn't* tell him! I *didn't*! I *didn't*! But your
luggage was gone and he twisted my arm—he twisted and
twisted . . .

(BROWNING *moves* R *of Arabel,* HENRIETTA *moves* L *of Elizabeth*)

TICKET COLLECTOR (*astounded*) So help me . . .
ARABEL (*sobbing*) It hurt so dreadfully!
TICKET COLLECTOR. I never so much as laid a finger on the
lady . . .

(*The* BROTHERS *run on up* R, *followed grimly by* BARRETT)

ARABEL (*running upstage to* Wilson) Don't let him come near
me! Don't let him come near me!

(*The* MELOS *stops. They come to the following positions:* -*Upstage,
from* R *to* L; GEORGE, CHARLES, OCTAVIUS: *extreme upstage* L,
WILSON, ARABEL; *downstage, from* R *to* L; ALFRED, SEPTIMUS,
HENRY, BARRETT, BROWNING, ELIZABETH, HENRIETTA, COOK.
BROWNING *deliberately comes between Barrett and Elizabeth*)

BROWNING. Good evening, Mr Barrett.
BARRETT. I have only one thing to say to you. Abduction is a
criminal offence. I shall see you pay the full price for it. Now
get out of my way.
BROWNING (*with a smile*) Abduction? Did you say abduction?
GEORGE. It's not particularly funny, Browning.
CHARLES. No, Ba, you can't run off with him like this.
HENRY. Not the way to do it, old girl.
ALFRED. Not done.
SEPTIMUS. Create a scandal.
OCTAVIUS. Who c-cares about a scandal?
ELIZABETH (*coming forward; quietly*) Thank you, Occy. But
there's no scandal. Father, this is my husband.
GEORGE. *He's dead!*
BARRETT (*at length; stunned*) You're lying.
HENRIETTA (*moving* L *of Elizabeth*) No, Father, she's not. They
were married at Marylebone Church. I've seen the register—
September the twelfth, eighteen forty-six. Look, here's the ring.
(*She indicates the ring on Elizabeth's left hand*)

BROWNING. And now—I don't know if anyone would care to wish us luck?
THE BROTHERS. Good Lord! Married! Well, I'm damned! T-t-terrific, etc.

(*The* BROTHERS *all crowd in to congratulate Elizabeth and* BROWNING. *Everyone then moves up to the train, leaving* BROWNING *and* BARRETT *facing each other. After a moment* BROWNING *moves to the train, and* ELIZABETH *comes downstage to* BARRETT. WILSON *and* EVANS *get into the train. The* GUARD *enters, blowing a final whistle, his green flag poised. Doors slam, there are last-minute farewells.* ELIZABETH *turns to Barrett, appealingly, with a final plea for his blessing)*

BROWNING (*from the carriage steps, as every door but theirs is shut*) Elizabeth!
ELIZABETH (*to Barrett, her arms open; hopefully*) Papa . . .?

(BARRETT *makes no move to touch her or to allow himself to be touched, but turns his head away in stony silence. The* GUARD *raises his flag)*

BROWNING (*moving down towards Elizabeth*) Elizabeth!

ELIZABETH *gives a last, lingering look at Barrett, then turns to join Browning.* BROWNING *and* ELIZABETH *run through the rising steam to their carriage.* BROWNING *helps her into the train and slams the door. The* GUARD *drops his flag. The train pulls out, leaving* HENRIETTA, ARABEL, COOK *and the* BROTHERS *in a group waving —and the solitary figure of* BARRETT *alone, apart, completely isolated, as—*

the LIGHTS *fade*

REPRISES

No. 30

The train goes off L. *A model of the train is seen crossing from* L *to* R *behind a gauze. Suddenly, almost before we are aware it has happened, the* MUSIC *resolves to a reprise of "The Moon in My Pocket", and we are in—*

SCENE 8

Florence Station

The station is all light and colour and noble architecture, with the bright Italian hills broadly visible in the background.

As the LIGHTS *come up, a* CROWD *in gay Italian clothes is milling on the platform, among them a* GUARD. *A train, gleaming and new, puffs into the station* RC. *The crowd are pushed back* L *and* R. *The* GUARD *opens the carriage door.* BROWNING *and* ELIZABETH, *now in the gayest of clothes and the gayest of moods, alight, followed by* Evans, Wilson *and* Flush. *The crowd welcomes them and from it, to* Elizabeth's *amazement and delight, emerges* Dr Chambers. Elizabeth *moves to greet* Chambers LC, *then joins* Browning C. *The* Music *leads into a reprise of "I know now".*

Ensemble (*singing*)
    And so now
    When they say heaven's far away
    If there is truth in what they say
    There must be two
Elizabeth *and* Browning (*singing together*)
    The one that's far away above
    The one that's having you to love
    My whole life through
Ensemble.   This I know now
    And so, I know, do you!

And with Robert *and* Elizabeth *safely in Italy—and each other's arms—*
    the Curtain *falls*

CURTAIN CALLS   No. 31

After the Curtain Calls, *a final chorus is sung by the* Entire Company *to the melody which opened the play—*

FINALE   No. 32

Browning, Elizabeth *and* Full Ensemble (*singing together*)
    Rain may be falling on Wimpole Street
    Oxford Street and Cavendish Square
    Here it's a perfectly splendid day
    Light and gay
    With love in the air
    And lovers to spare
Men.   Lovely lady
Women.   Handsome hero
Ensemble.   Happy ending
    Final Curtain
    Is waiting to fall
    On circle and stall
    They're closing the hall
    Good night to you all!

FURNITURE AND PROPERTY PLOT

ACT I
SCENE I

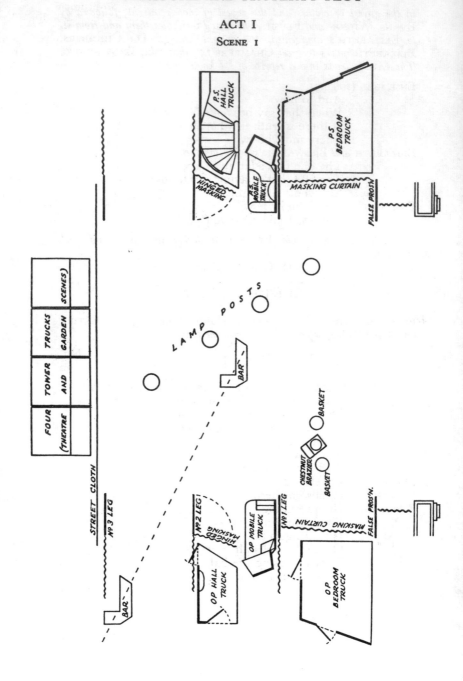

On stage: 4 lamp-posts
Chestnut brazier (R), *Beside it:* tray of chestnuts, basket of
fruit, basket of tomatoes
Off stage: Lamplighter (LAMPLIGHTER)
Street broom (SWEEPER)
9 prayer-books (BARRETT FAMILY)
Bar with tankards (BARMAID)
Dartboard and darts on stand (LAMPLIGHTER)
Personal: ELEGANT GENTLEMAN: wallet
2 ELEGANT LADIES: purses

SCENE 2

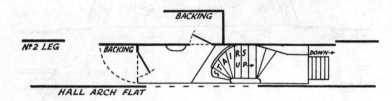

Act I Scene 2 and 6. Act II Scene 2 and 4

On stage: Harmonium (down R). *On it:* music
Stool (above harmonium)
Seat (R)
Small table or shelf (up C). *On it:* CHAMBERS' hat and gloves,
silver salver with 6 sealed letters
Seat (above fire L)

Seat (below fire L). *On it:* embroidery frame with needle and
silk
Stool (down L)
Carpet
Off stage: 2 hall chairs (HENRY, ALFRED)
Chess-board and pieces (HENRY, ALFRED)
Medical bag (CHAMBERS)

SCENE 3

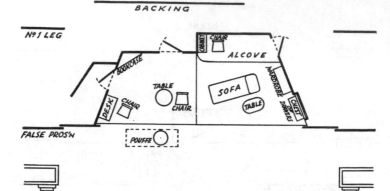

Act I Scene 3 and 5. Act II Scene 1 and 5

On stage: Desk table (down R). *On it:* oil lamp, quill pen, writing
paper, rack, azalea in pot
Table (C). *On it:* playing cards laid out, fan
Bookcase (up R). *In shelves:* practical books
Dresser (down L). *On it:* bowl of sweets
Sofa (RC). *On it:* rug, supper tray with plate of food, knife,
fork, tankard
Table (below sofa). *On it:* opened letter
Table (in alcove). *On it:* portable writing desk with pen and
paper, smelling salts
Chair (at desk)
Chair (L of C table)
Chair (in alcove)
Four-poster bed (in alcove)
Pedestal (C). *On it:* oil lamp
Off stage: Tankard of porter (HENRIETTA)

SCENE 4

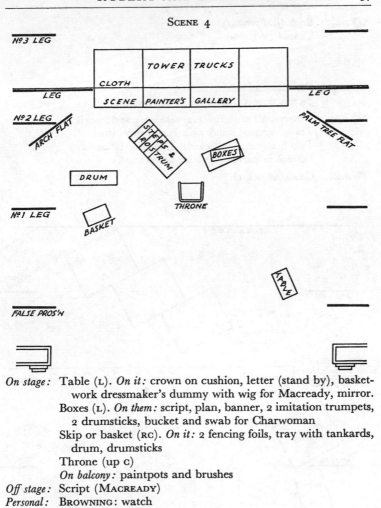

On stage: Table (L). *On it:* crown on cushion, letter (stand by), basket-
work dressmaker's dummy with wig for Macready, mirror.
Boxes (L). *On them:* script, plan, banner, 2 imitation trumpets,
2 drumsticks, bucket and swab for Charwoman
Skip or basket (RC). *On it:* 2 fencing foils, tray with tankards,
drum, drumsticks
Throne (up C)
On balcony: paintpots and brushes
Off stage: Script (MACREADY)
Personal: BROWNING: watch
EVANS: letter in hat

SCENE 5

On stage: Furniture as before
Pouffe (down C)
Under sofa: 2 pills
Under desk: 2 pills
On table below sofa: tray with 2 cups and saucers, plate of
teacakes, 3 spoons, 2 knives, sugar, milk, tumbler of water,
box of pills
Under C table: 2 pills
On C table: fan

Off stage: Book (BROWNING)
Teapot (WILSON)

SCENE 6

On stage: Furniture as before
On seat down L: newspaper (for Barrett)

Off stage: Flower-stall with flowers, notebook and pencil
Travel agency stand with ITALY brochure
Two bouquets with cards (UNSEEN MESSENGER)
Parasol in parcel (UNSEEN MESSENGER)

Personal: CHARLES: watch

SCENE 7

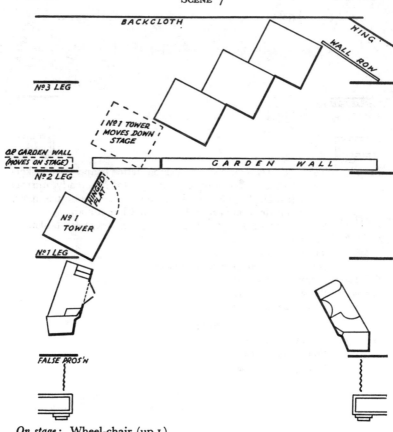

On stage: Wheel-chair (up L)
Wicker chair (up R)

ACT II

SCENE 1

On stage: Furniture as before
            On sofa table: tankard, opened letter
            On dresser: Eau de Cologne

SCENE 2

On stage: Furniture as before
            On mantelpiece: cigar case
            On stool down L: "Blackwood's Magazine"
            On table up C: Barrett's hat and gloves
            In stick holder: Barrett's walking-stick
Off stage: Pile of 4 dress-boxes (ARABEL)
            1 small hatbox (BELLA)
            Barrett's frock-coat (CHARLES)
            Barrett's overcoat (ALFRED)
Personal: BELLA: handbag with mirror

SCENE 3

On stage: Brazier and tray of chestnuts (up L)
Winkle stall with bowls and winkles (down L)
Drinks table with glasses, bottles (up R)
Wicker chair (up R)
Wicker chair (down R)
Wicker table (down R). *On it:* pen and paper (for Browning)
Sandwich board (for Sandwich-board Man)

SCENE 4

On stage: Furniture as before, except:
Dressing struck
Other items covered with dust-sheets
On floor down C: tin trunk, packed, lid open

SCENE 5

On stage: Furniture as before
On desk: books, including Baedeker

SCENE 6

Act 2 Scene 6 and 7

Act I Sc. 4

Act II Sc. 3

Act II Sc. 6

Act II Sc. 8

Act I Sc. 1

Act I Sc. 2

Act I Sc. 2 and 6, Act II Sc. 2 and 4

Act I Sc. 3 and 5, Act II Sc. 1 and 5

On stage: Rustic table (L). *On it:* 2 books, salver, decanter and glass
Swivel chair (L)
Off stage: Letter (EVANS)

SCENE 7

On stage: Train (L)
Barrier (up C)
On platform: mailbags
Off stage: 2 small trunks (EVANS)
Hatbox (BROWNING)
Mailbags (PORTER)
Whistle, green flag (GUARD)
Personal: BROWNING: coins
ELIZABETH: wedding ring

SCENE 8

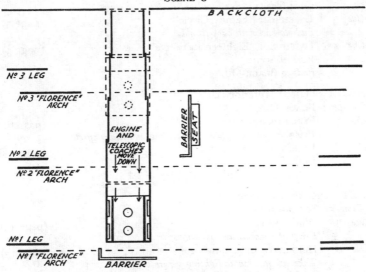

On stage: Train (R)

Character Costumes and wigs used in the performance of plays
contained in French's Acting Edition may be obtained from
Messrs CHARLES H. FOX LTD, 184 High Holborn, London, W.C.1

LIGHTING PLOT

Property fittings required:
4 street lamps (Act I Scene 1)
Gas brackets, 2 oil lamps (ELIZABETH's Room scenes)
Fairy lights (Act II Scene 3)
Special lighting for model train (Act II Scenes 7–8)

ACT I SCENE 1. Exterior. Evening
To open: Effect of early dusk. General lighting
Cue 1   LADIES: "The only ones there"   (page 2)
         Build up light on Bar c
Cue 2   LAD: "Especially Clare"   (page 3)
         Cross-fade to concentrate light on front of stage
Cue 3   ENSEMBLE: "Family Circle"   (page 5)
         Fade to backcloth back lit only
Cue 4   ENSEMBLE: "Eighteen forty-five"   (page 5)
         End of Scene
         Fade to BLACK-OUT

ACT I SCENE 2. Interior. Day
To open: BLACK-OUT
Cue 5   When ready   (page 6)
         Bring up general lighting, depressing and heavy effect
Cue 6   ENSEMBLE: "West one!"   (page 13)
         End of Scene
         Fade to BLACK-OUT

ACT I SCENE 3. Interior. Night
To open: BLACK-OUT
Cue 7   When ready   (page 13)
         Bring up brackets and oil lamps
Cue 8   HENRIETTA turns down gas   (page 17)
         Take out gas, reduce lighting generally
Cue 9   BARRETT turns out lamp R   (page 20)
         Take out lamp R *and all lighting except spot*
         covering lamp c
Cue 10   ELIZABETH starts to write   (page 20)
         End of Scene
         Fade to BLACK-OUT

ACT I SCENE 4. Interior. An empty stage
To open: BLACK-OUT
Cue 11   When ready   (page 21)
         Bring up to general, fairly bright, lighting
Cue 12   BROWNING and ENSEMBLE: "All's right with the
         world!"   (page 27)
         End of Scene
         Fade to BLACK-OUT

ACT I Scene 5. Interior (as Scene 3). Afternoon
To open: BLACK-OUT
Cue 13   When ready   (page 27)
          Bring up to same lighting as Cue 7
Cue 14   BROWNING and ELIZABETH: ". . . here in my
              heart"   (page 39)
          End of Scene
          Fade to BLACK-OUT

ACT I Scene 6. Interior (as Scene 2)
To open: BLACK-OUT
Cue 15   When ready   (page 39)
          Bring up to same lighting as Cue 5
Cue 16   WILSON: "Dear Lord!"   (page 39)
          Cross-fade to spot on Flower Stall down L
Cue 17   BROWNING: ". . . household word"   (page 40)
          Cross-fade to opening lighting
Cue 18   BARRETT stares upstairs   (page 40)
          Fade to BLACK-OUT
Cue 19   Immediately following   (page 40)
          Bring up opening lighting
Cue 20   WILSON: ". . . asked for a steak!"   (page 40)
          Snap BLACK-OUT
Cue 21   Immediately following   (page 40)
          Bring up to opening lighting
Cue 22   HENRIETTA: "Love me now!"   (page 41)
          Fade to BLACK-OUT
Cue 23   When ready   (page 41)
          Bring up spot on Travel Agency
Cue 24   BROWNING walks upstage from Travel Agency   (page 41)
          Cross-fade to opening lighting
Cue 25   ARABEL faints   (page 41)
          Snap BLACK-OUT
Cue 26   When ready   (page 41)
          Bring up to opening lighting
Cue 27   CHAMBERS opens french window   (page 41)
          Bring up sunlight inside and outside
Cue 28   BARRETT carries ELIZABETH into garden   (page 42)
          Cross-fade into sundrenched garden as scene changes
                              OR
          Fade to BLACK-OUT

ACT I Scene 7. Exterior. Daylight
          NOTE If revolving set is used, omit following
              Black-out opening and *Cue* 29. Continue from
              Cue 30
To open: BLACK-OUT
Cue 29   When ready   (page 42)
          Bring up to bright sunshine all over

Cue 30   ELIZABETH and BROWNING: "And so, I know,
        do you"   (page 53)
        Slight check of general lighting

ACT II SCENE 1. Interior (as Act I Scene 3). Evening
To open: Lamps on. Brackets low.
Cue 31   HENRIETTA turns up gas   (page 57)
        Bring up to same lighting as Cue 7
Cue 32   ALL: "Shoot!"   (page 61)
        End of Scene
        Fade to BLACK-OUT

ACT II SCENE 2. Interior (as Act I Scene 2)
To open: BLACK-OUT
Cue 33   When ready   (page 61)
        Bring up to same lighting as Cue 5
Cue 34   BROTHERS: "You're the Master here"   (page 69)
        End of Scene
        Snap BLACK-OUT

ACT II SCENE 3. Exterior. Night
To open: BLACK-OUT
Cue 35   When ready   (page 69)
        Bring up to bright moonlight, fairy lights
Cue 36   BROWNING: "No one I know, now"   (page 71)
        Fireworks effect
Cue 37   BROWNING: ". . . on his natal day"   (page 71)
        Fireworks effect
Cue 38   BROWNING: "I've no idea"   (page 72)
        Fireworks effect
Cue 39   HENRIETTA: "Good-bye forever"   (page 75)
        Fireworks effect
Cue 40   BROWNING: "That you've broken the spell!"   (page 78)
        End of Scene
        Snap BLACK-OUT

ACT II SCENE 4. Interior (as Act I Scene 2)
To open: BLACK-OUT
Cue 41   When ready   (page 78)
        Bring up to same lighting as Cue 5
Cue 42   HENRIETTA and COOK exit   (page 80)
        End of Scene
        Fade to BLACK-OUT

ACT II SCENE 5. Interior (as Act I Scene 3)
To open: BLACK-OUT
Cue 43   When ready   (page 80)
        Bring up to same lighting as Cue 7
Cue 44   BARRETT exits   (page 85)
        End of Scene
        Fade to BLACK-OUT

ACT II SCENE 6. Exterior. Evening
To open: BLACK-OUT
Cue 45   When ready   (page 86)
            Bring up to effect of early evening shadowy sunlight
Cue 46   BROWNING: "And Man is not!"   (page 88)
            End of Scene
            Snap BLACK-OUT

ACT II SCENE 7. Exterior. Day
To open: BLACK-OUT
Cue 47   When ready   (page 88)
            Bring up to murky railway station light
Cue 48   Train starts to leave   (page 92)
            Fade to spot on BARRETT *at* C
Cue 49   Immediately following   (page 92)
            Fade to BLACK-OUT
            NOTE: During Black-out the model train
               crosses stage from L to R

ACT II SCENE 8. Exterior. Day
To open: BLACK-OUT
Cue 50   When model train has crossed   (page 92)
            Bring up to bright, gay sunshine over entire stage

EFFECTS PLOT

ACT I

SCENE 2

Cue 1   BARRETT exits upstairs   (page 9)
Door slam

SCENE 3

Cue 2   At height of BROTHERS' brawl   (page 16)
Knocking on ceiling

SCENE 6

Cue 3   Lights come up after WILSON: ". . . for a steak!"   (page 40)
Knock on front door

Cue 4   Lights come up after ARABEL faints   (page 41)
Knock on front door

ACT II

SCENE 3

Cue 5   BROWNING: "No one I know—now"   (page 71)
Fireworks

Cue 6   BROWNING: ". . . on his natal day"   (page 71)
Fireworks

Cue 7   BROWNING: "I've no idea"   (page 72)
Fireworks

Cue 8   HENRIETTA: "Good-bye forever"   (page 75)
Fireworks, short burst

SCENE 6

Cue 9   BROWNING: ". . . of yellow gloves"   (page 87)
Knock on front door

SCENE 7

Cue 10   GUARD blows whistle   (page 92)
Rising steam from train

Cue 11   After Black-out   (page 92)
Model TRAIN travels across stage

SIMPLIFIED RUNNING SEQUENCE

(ACT I)

SCENE 1   The Vicinity of Wimpole Street
(full stage exterior)
At Wilson's entrance (music No 2, bar 218)
Close running tabs.
Play the rest of Scene 1 in front of tabs.
Set Hallway.
At end of music No 2
Open running tabs.

SCENE 2   The Hallway of 50 Wimpole Street
(three-quarter stage interior)
During scene:
Take out Wimpole Street backcloth
Drop in Theatre Royal backcloth
At "Onward Moulton Barrett" (music No 4, bar 117)
Cast moves DS
Close running tabs.
Play the rest of Scene 2 in front of tabs.
Set Bedroom (in front of Hallway)
At end of music No 4, and during No 4A
Open running tabs.

SCENE 3   Elizabeth's Bedroom
(half stage interior)
During scene:
Strike Hallway
Set Theatre Royal
At end of Scene 3
Close running tabs.

SCENE 4   Theatre Royal, Haymarket
(open in front of running tabs.
Go to full stage interior when ready)
As scene opens:
Strike Bedroom
When Bedroom struck
Open running tabs.
At "Trumpets Ring Out" (music No 9, Figure 'o')
Cast moves DS
Close running tabs.
Play the rest of Scene 4 in front of tabs.

Set Bedroom
At ends of music No 9
Open running tabs.

SCENE 5   Elizabeth's Bedroom
(half stage interior)
During scene:
Set Hallway
Take out Theatre Royal backcloth
Drop in Wimpole Street backcloth
Set Wimpole Street Garden behind Hallway
At end of music No 13
Close running tabs.
Strike Bedroom
(if necessary, at this point BROWNING can move in front of
running tabs and reprise music No 13 as a solo)
When Bedroom struck
Open running tabs.

SCENE 6   The Hallway
(three-quarter stage interior—
with Episodes in acting area spots extreme DL and DR)
In the absence of a revolve:
Immediately after DOCTOR CHAMBERS has opened the door
to the garden (music No 13, bar 220) BARRETT appears on
the stairs with ELIZABETH in his arms. As the FAMILY watch,
he carries her through the open garden door. DOCTOR
CHAMBERS then moves DS
Close running tabs.
DOCTOR CHAMBERS continues his solo in front of tabs.
Strike Hallway
Complete setting Garden
At music No 13, bar 267
Open running tabs.
BARRETT now enters to the Garden, carrying ELIZABETH.

SCENE 7   The Garden of 50 Wimpole Street
(full stage exterior)
Remain to end of Act 1
During Interval:
Strike Garden
Drop in Cremorne Gardens backcloth
Set Hallway
Set Bedroom (in front of Hallway)

(ACT II)

SCENE 1   Elizabeth's Bedroom
(half stage interior)
At end of music No 19 (Blackout)
Close running tabs.
(The orchestra has covering music at this point. An extra
20/30 seconds can be obtained for this change by bringing the
Cast DS at "All hail our darling sister!", music No 19,
bar 120, and *Closing* running tabs, but this should be avoided
if at all possible.)
During scene change music:
Strike Bedroom
When Bedroom struck
Open running tabs

SCENE 2   The Hallway
(three-quarter stage interior)
At "Right is wrong", (music No 21, Figure "E")
Cast moves DS
Close running tabs.
Play the rest of Scene 2 in front of tabs.
Strike Hallway
Set Cremorne Gardens

SCENE 3   Cremorne Gardens, Chelsea
(if necessary, open—with the arrival of some of the visitors to
the Gardens—in front of tunning tabs. Go to full stage
exterior when ready)
When ready
Open running tabs.

SCENE 4   The Hallway
(For this short scene it is possible to omit the return to the
Hallway set. The Barretts are packing in preparation for
leaving Wimpole Street. By setting a trunk, a packing case
and a long stool in front of the running tabs, and using
acting area spots rather than full lighting, it can be suggested
that the packing is continuing, well into the evening, in a
part of the ground floor of 50 Wimpole Street which we
have not previously visited.
If this simplification is adopted, BROWNING's entrance
becomes a cross-over, from R to L. COOK appears at extreme
DR and HENRIETTA crosses to him there. The other mem-
bers of the FAMILY exit L & R, taking the properties with
them)
During scene:
Strike Cremorne Gardens

Set Bedroom
Set Vauxhall Station (behind Bedroom)
Set Train for Florence Arrival and Finale
   At end of Scene 4
   Open running tabs.

SCENE 5   Elizabeth's Bedroom
   (half stage interior)
      At end of Scene 5
      Drop in front-cloth

SCENE 6   Outside Browning's Study
   (front-drop)
   During scene:
   Strike Bedroom
      At end of Scene 6
      Take out front-drop

SCENE 7/8 Vauxhall Station, Train Journey, and Florence Arrival
   (composite full stage exterior)
      Remain to end of Act II